WHY YOU CAN'T BEAT *WALL STREET*

THE LOSING GAME

T.E. Scott
written with Stephen Edds

Hidden Truth Publishing
Rockville, Indiana

The Losing Game: Why You Can't Beat Wall Street
T.E. Scott
Written with Stephen Edds

Published by Hidden Truth Publishing
P.O. Box 168
Rockville, IN 47872
www.losinggame.com

ISBN: 978-0-9819370-3-8
Library of Congress Control Number: 2008941316
This book is printed on acid-free paper.
Printed in the United States of America

Illustrations by John Marr

About the Authors

T.E. Scott founded and spent twenty-five years as CEO of a multi-million dollar pet supply products manufacturer in Indiana. Before starting that business, Scott spent thirty-two years working for Eastern Airlines. He lost most of his pension when the company went bankrupt in the 1980s. He and his late wife started selling dog leads and collars out of their home and built their enterprise into a multimillion-dollar company in Rockville, Indiana. Scott is retired and has spent the last several years developing the ideas and concepts for this book. Scott resides in Veedersburg, Indiana. *www.losinggame.com*

Stephen Edds is a native of Owensboro, Kentucky and is a graduate of Hanover (Indiana) College. Edds spent fifteen years in corporate marketing communications before striking out on his own as a freelance writer. Edds moved to Indianapolis in 1996, where he still resides with his wife, Erin, and son Levi. *www.stephenedds.com*

Table of Contents

Foreword

You should be outraged.

You should know better.

You should be storming the Capitol demanding reform.

But you're not outraged.

And you don't know better.

Neither did I, until recently.

When I met T.E. Scott, I was a struggling freelance writer, working in a nightmare corporate job and looking for a way out. My knowledge of the stock market and Wall Street, like that of many college graduates, was painfully incomplete. So, when the opportunity was presented to write a book on the stock market, I jumped at the chance.

When T.E. explained the premise of the book, my initial reaction to my role as a coauthor would be similar to that of a defense attorney. I didn't necessarily need to understand or believe my client—I just needed to present the best case for him.

Over the course of several months, I made many trips to Veedersburg, Indiana, to capture his thoughts on paper. We had vigorous debates, where I challenged his beliefs and he challenged mine. Meanwhile, I began to study the markets to see if I could find any corresponding evidence. Then it sank in . . . he's onto something.

I bombarded T.E. with articles, books and news reports to lend support to his ideas. I believed that once people read the facts, they would better understand his argument. T.E. didn't want that, though. He didn't want to clutter his message. He kept telling me, "We have got to keep it simple."

The Losing Game is T.E. Scott's straightforward view of how we've been conditioned to play a losing game when we start placing our trust and our money in the markets. Based on his experiences, thoughts and observations, this book is direct, brief and to the point.

Those of you expecting a PhD-level academic explanation of how the markets work won't find it here. We're not investment advisors, so what you do with your money is up to you. Those of you looking for a way to "beat the system" won't find it here either. (Here's a hint: You can't.)

The main emphasis of the book is on getting you to rethink a concept you've accepted without question your entire life. We want the people who are losing money in the markets to quit losing and demand accountability from those in charge of managing your money. It's a formidable task to be sure, but the alternative is far worse.

Revolutions are not started by those in power. Revolutions begin with someone who has had enough, who has nothing left to lose. In T.E. Scott's case, it took losing his pension and starting over from scratch to spur a self-made entrepreneur in west-central Indiana with little formal education to question the very foundation of the American economy and figure out that it is a losing game for all but a very few.

T.E. Scott has nothing to lose. You, on the other hand, have your retirement and pension to lose. You have the power to decide if the system we support should remain in place. If you are outraged, then together we can make our voices heard, demanding real accountability and bringing a corrupt system to its knees.

Hopefully, we change a corrupt system for the better.

—Stephen Edds
September, 2008

Introduction

My name is T.E. Scott, and this book was written to expose the stock market and commodity markets as the two largest ongoing scams in United States history. Like many of you, I was a victim of this scam as an employee at Eastern Airlines. I worked as a baggage handler for thirty-two years and was given "preferred stock" as part of my pay package. Funny thing is, when the company went bankrupt, my stock must have been "preferred" because they took it first. As a result, I lost three-quarters of my pension.

I was lucky: I had started my own business in my living room and through sheer determination managed to build that into a very successful, privately owned company in west-central Indiana. But I never forgot what guys like Frank Lorenzo at Eastern Airlines did to me and 45,000 thousand of my coworkers. But more important, I kept seeing it happening to average people every day, not only at Enron and World Com but to the people I talked to where I live in Indiana. People were getting ripped off in the markets and had no

voice or recourse. Amazingly enough, some even thought it was their own fault.

I began thinking about the true nature of investments and how they're presented to us as opposed to what they really are. It should be a good deal only when all parties benefit. And yet, when you take a close look at the markets, there are no circumstances when all parties benefit. I also figured out that in a fair investment situation, 5 percent net is a reasonable return on a cash investment. It's not sexy to promote a 5 percent investment as a good one, but believe me, when you're done with this book, you'll happily take that.

Have no doubt, some people make fortunes in the markets, but that money has to come from somewhere. Or more specifically, from someone. The market by its very definition is an "exchange" where shares of stock or commodities contracts are "traded." If people are making money, then other people are losing money. Who precisely is losing the money that all the people are making? No one was asking that question, and I felt someone needed to.

For the past four years I've been thinking, talking, listening, and debating with people about the function of the stock and commodities markets. I've studied how investments should work and how the markets actually work, and I have come to the unmistakable conclusion that the average American is getting fleeced and pillaged every day, and we're letting it happen.

We have been conned for decades by a system set up by the heads of Wall Street's brokerage houses, bankers, brokers and money managers. I call them "masters of illusion and deception" because they are experts in devising business plans, marketing campaigns and lobbying efforts to keep their business profitable and legal, despite never producing a single tangible product. They've been masters at creating new revenue streams under the guise of "investing" and masters at drawing more and more investors in using illusions and deceptions.

I'm not the only one who believes this. John C. Bogle, founder of the Vanguard Group, says stockholders have been part of a "Happy Conspiracy" consisting of corporate executives, auditors, Wall Street bankers, analysts and informed shareholders, all taking advantage of a naïve, uninformed investing public. According to Bogle, their shared goal has been creating a rising stock price.

Former Richard Nixon strategist Kevin Phillips, author of *The Politics of the Rich & the Poor*, described America as a plutocracy, where government is controlled by the wealthy elite.

It makes sense, doesn't it? It's mutually beneficial for politicians, financial leaders and the media for Wall Street to be perceived to be doing well. Therefore, these interests will work to present a view of the markets that is counter to the truth.

Through the years, Wall Street's power brokers have proven to be brilliant, greedy, powerful, influential, and addicted to wealth without remorse. A few may be without a conscience, but most are just greedy, and a great many may be blissfully ignorant of the con.

I wonder if they initially were motivated to seek wealth to accumulate power, or did they seek power to accumulate wealth? Maybe they're intertwined, but the one thing I'm certain of is they have targeted you as their prey.

You have been conned by Wall Street. To be clear, I mean "Wall Street" that describes the financial services industry and not a street in lower Manhattan. To fully understand how and why this has happened, one of the hardest things you'll have to do is ignore the information, advice, and the conditioning that you've accepted without question. Don't believe that the markets ever have or ever will be working in your best interest.

The Losing Game will simplify a very complex system that Wall Street has designed, developed, and perfected over time to separate the masses from their money without accountability or prosecution. As a result of this design, the power brokers have tricked us into believing that the stock market and commodity markets are something they are not.

One way Wall Street did this while avoiding scrutiny was to design the system to be so complex that very few fully understand it. To keep from getting tangled in their web of confusion and keep this simple, we will focus on the basics of the markets. This will prevent you from getting distracted by excess language that merely adds confusion to any understanding of the markets. As a result, there are no sections addressing options, hedge funds, indexing, selling short or long, because the results are the same—it's all gambling, and it's all a scam.

Plus no matter how complicated they make it, the basics are still the same . . . you are participating in a minus-sum gambling game. If I wrote a thousand-page book about the complexities of the system, the economic elite might praise it, and yet most of you would understand what's happening no more or less than you do now.

Now, how did a high-school educated, common man like me figure all this out? Through my work, I began to see through the illusions and deceptions used to distract us and started to ask simple questions of those considering participating in the markets:

- Where does the money come from when an investor makes money?
- Where does the money go when an investor loses his or her money?
- Why aren't any financial records kept to track investors' money?

- Why are brokers and money managers not required to produce records of how much money their clients lose?
- Why isn't the industry as a whole required to provide full disclosure and accountability of investors' money?
- Who actually controls the stock market and commodities markets?
- Why doesn't anyone question the real role of the regulatory commissions?

By asking these questions, and actively seeking answers, I figured out that Wall Street operators had hidden the truth of their motives, while covering themselves in countless disclaimers.

Like magicians, these Wall Streeters who control the markets create a spectacular show to distract you from the simple sleight-of-hand they are performing. No magician truthfully says he can saw a woman in half and then put her back together again. But you want to believe he can. The magicians do it for entertainment; Wall Street does it to separate you from your money.

A vast majority of investors lose money in the stock markets and commodity markets. The exact number is impossible to determine because those statistics are not kept, nor are they required to be kept. Think about that for a moment. Wall Street controls TRILLIONS of dollars of your money, and are not required to keep records tracking your money. If that is not a recipe for greed and fraud, I don't know what is.

I drew my own conclusions based on my evaluation of the system, but I do know for sure that the markets are a minus-sum game for average investors. More than 50 percent lose money just because of the way the markets are designed. If you factor in the added advantages that the select few insiders enjoy and consider the number of companies that leave investors holding the bag when the shares are removed from trading, the percentages increase significantly. With 95 million investors currently in the markets, a safe estimate is that 48 million people are losing money. And that is the LOW number, it could be much higher.

I will point out throughout the book that the exchanges and brokers do not keep these records. The government does not require them, the media don't ask for them, the brokers and exchanges don't keep them, and investors take the brokers at their word without question. Until someone can show a full accounting of total investors as a whole instead of a hand-picked few, how can you trust a financial system cloaked in secrecy?

Early on, I figured out investors are simply players in the gambling games Wall Street developed. Therefore, to keep it simple, I will refer to investors, traders, hedgers, speculators and clients as "investors." I also ask you to not look at individual successes, but look at all investors as a whole to get a complete view of the markets. Looking at the success of a few people in the markets is playing into the hands of Wall Street. You would not look at the winner of the lottery jackpot as a representative of all lottery participants as a whole, nor should you with investors in the market.

Wall Street has you believing the illusion that you will make money by playing the markets and that the success of the markets is vital to the success of the economy. The deception is that those involved in your investments are working strictly in the best interest of you as an investor. They've convinced you that participating in the market is a sound financial strategy vital to a strong economy. This is a lie.

Here's the fact: The total existence of the markets revolves around constantly changing prices and selling by the second to create motion. This constant motion takes money out of the pockets of investors and puts it in the pockets of a select few. If all investors play long enough, they will all lose money in time.

I can't stress enough that motion is the primary goal of everyone in any management level involved in your financial planning. This process keeps the markets functioning because it takes real cash from your pockets and replaces it with a piece of paper with published value, which is worthless unless you find someone else to buy it. Either way, they still have your money.

Despite all of the books, newsletters, analysts, and seminars that tell you how to beat the system, if all things were equal, all investors will lose money in time. My goal with *The Losing Game* is simply to get you to quit losing money. It's impossible for investors as a whole to beat the markets. The only way to get you to quit losing is for you to quit participating. The great thing about this is that you in control. This is one area in which we don't need our politicians to enact a federal law. If you quit losing money, the markets in theory will correct themselves.

The problem is that Wall Street is so intertwined with Congress that they can make poor decisions, bad investments and business decisions, and pressure Washington for a trillion-dollar bailout that essentially "double-dips" from the American people. They mismanaged your investment, and now they want your tax money to bail them out? Outrageous!

What I am presenting in *The Losing Game* will not be popular with those who continue to profit by maintaining the status quo. They will attack me and attempt to discredit me by presenting anecdotal or incomplete information on individual successes to convince you that the system may not work for everyone, but it can work for you.

They will tell you about the risk of investing but not offer specifics. They will tell you that educated investors are successful investors but offer no concrete proof. They will tell you that they made money but, when asked who that money came from, will answer, "I don't care."

More importantly, they will claim, as they did during the bailout debate, that they perform a vital function in the American economy, and their failure spells doom for the American and even worldwide economy. This is simply not true.

By exposing the illusions and deceptions Wall Street used in designing their business model, I will show you some simple facts:

- The stock market and commodity markets are gambling facilities, no more and no less.

- Wall Street firms use weak words, the manipulation of statistics, lack of statistics, and psychological tricks to convince you that you are doing something other than gambling.

- Investing in the markets is a minus-sum game, which means that at the end of the day, investors wind up with less money than they started with.

- *Published value, perceived value,* and *outperformed* are terms of illusion and deception that give you a false perception of actual value.

- Wall Street firms, brokers and money managers are not working in your best interests, and they capitalize on your ignorance of the markets to make as much money for them, not you, as possible.

- You can't beat the system. If all things were equal, all investors would lose money in time.

I will not allow you to be trapped in their web by letting them focus on the "eagle's eye view," which focuses on the success or failure of specific individuals. Instead I'll show you why the markets are a minus-sum game to investors as a whole and explain why you shouldn't be involved.

My critics will dismiss my simple approach as someone who "doesn't get it," and I will be rejected as a "conspiracy nut" in an effort to discredit me.

But the fact is countless books and articles address the flaws of the markets without pointing out that the entire system itself is flawed. And, unlike most other writers, I have not devised a way to beat the system, because there isn't a way.

The Losing Game will open your eyes so you can see that what you have been led to believe about Wall Street is a lie. You are part of an elaborate ongoing con game to separate you from your money. All I'm doing is exposing it as a gambling system for the average person to understand and, I hope, avoid. I'm presenting a case that provides a straightforward explanation of a system that was designed to overwhelm us.

For real change to take place and for my message to get out, I'll need your help. Together, we can empower you to take charge of your investment and retirement by exposing Wall Street's elaborate gambling setup which slowly robs you of your money.

It's only a losing game to those who choose to participate. Hopefully, after reading this book, you'll choose wisely.

WOULD YOU PLAY THIS GAME?

1

You Can't Beat the System

L et's make this easy. There's no way to beat the system. None. It doesn't exist. From the moment you start investing by buying a share of stock or commodity contract, you are participating in what I call a minus-sum game. At the end of the day, investors (you, your family, neighbors and coworkers) as a whole will lose money. That is not a theory, it's a simple fact!

What do I mean by a "minus-sum game?" If you think about it, investors are the only ones putting money into the pot through buying shares of stock or commodity contracts. When a company sells a share, it takes money out of the pot and does not give it back to the investors. Wall Street brokers and the stock market and commodities exchanges take a cut out of the investors' pot every time investors buy and sell thereafter. The company, brokers and exchanges are taking money out of the pot, and investors are the only ones putting money in. Investors as a whole will wind up with less money in hand at the end of the day than they started with. That should tell you right away that, if you're participating in a "minus-sum game," you can't beat the system.

Every day, people who put their hard-earned money into commodity market contracts and shares in publicly traded companies in the stock market lose billions of dollars to the exchanges, brokerage firms, IRS, money managers, company shares, CEO stock options, and other investors. The financial leaders who designed the system have developed a brilliant and successful business plan to separate the masses from their money without accountability or prosecution by creating legalized gambling. The rich and greedy who use this system to accumulate wealth and power without remorse have total control. The rest of us, the victims of their marketing scheme, are merely pawns. Now, you may believe you are investing when, in fact, you are playing complex minus-sum gambling games created to separate you from your money. You are gambling with your retirement, pensions and 401k, just as if you were at the slot machines at Las Vegas, except for one thing . . . Vegas is honest.

You can win only if you figure out a way to beat the system.

But let me repeat this: *You can't beat the system.* No mathematical or scientific formula exists that will make money for investors as a whole over time. It's impossible. You're attempting to predict an unpredictable, and your poor predictions keep the markets open. Like any casino, the markets promote the winners, but they need the losers' money to survive. It's a mathematical fact that investors wind up with less money at the end of every day than they started with. Investors are the only ones taking money out of their pockets and purchasing shares and contracts as part of the system. Brokers and exchanges are taking money out of the system and putting it in their pockets. It's important to remember that until you actually sell your stocks or cash in your 401 (k), that it's irrelevant how much your investment has grown or shrunk.

When a brokerage firm takes a risk on an investment, you can be guaranteed that they have access to information, legal and illegal, that average investors don't have. It gets worse when you factor in the advantages that the investor doesn't have. These include insider trading and information, CEO stock options, seats on the exchange, broker manipulation of stock prices, naked short-selling, and other factors. The fact that firms like Lehman Brothers, AIG, and Merrill Lynch are in trouble suggests that even with this information, they are gambling just as much, and in their case, lost heavily.

Why *The Losing Game* isn't promoting any way to "beat the system"

Simple: there isn't a way. You think there are ways, and people write and refer to books on how they and others have succeeded in the markets. But it's a lie. The honest fact is that many so-called "investment gurus" make far more money on their books, DVDs and seminars than they ever did in the stock market. They're famous for using the eagle's eye view to show a few examples where their systems made people money. However, here's the key: they don't show you complete statistics and don't provide a full accounting of investors' money, because they don't have to. They never show what would have happened if you had applied the system consistently. If you were to test these methods, you'll find that over time, none of them works. Why? It's a minus-sum game. The idea that any book, program, seminar, or broker can promote a winning system without providing illegal insider information is a waste of your money and energy. The few who make money are no more significant to you as an investor than your neighbor winning the lottery.

In fact, most of these "Wall Street Experts" make far more money from their books, CDs, DVDs and seminars than they ever would by applying their "can't miss" formulas in the markets.

The eagle's eye view

I use the eagle as an example because, when an eagle is soaring above the ground, it can see everything beneath it. However, when it sees its food, it focuses intently on only that, ignoring everything else around. This single-minded focus is a strength for the eagle hunting for a meal but a weakness for investors being deceived by brokers. By focusing on the eagle's eye view, brokers can draw on anecdotal evidence to show you individual cases to manipulate you to believe whatever it is they want to sell you. They won't tell you that the majority of investors lose money, and they won't produce a record of investors' money or where the money goes.

I've debated countless people who refuse to believe that Wall Street is a scam because they (singular) have made money. If they have made money, then they believe others haven't due to their own ignorance of the markets or simple greed. They refuse to believe that, like a casino, they were simply lucky and that eventually, the house always wins.

Wall Street does a brilliant job in promoting the eagle's eye view in discussing the advantages of the markets. They will encourage the ongoing success of certain funds, or prop up the success of certain analysts, or create a reporting system that reflects only the performance of a select few stocks, which are constantly changing to reflect the best stocks. They use incomplete information and manipulate statistics, which they can use to show great wealth and success to the select few that follow their complex system. But at the end of the day, it doesn't change the fact that you can't beat the system.

Let's look at the charts below. All four are simple examples of what would happen if you purchased stock in a publicly traded company.

Example 1: Investor A purchased a share of stock from a company for $100

Out of pocket money...*In pocket money*
- Investor A $100...................sells to Investor B for $110
- Investor B $110...................sells to Investor C for $120
- Investor C $120................. sells to Investor D for $130
- Investor D $130

Total out of pocket.......................................$–460

Total in-pocket $360

Total out of pocket..................................... –$100

Investor	Paid out	Sold for	Investor's gain (or loss)
A	$100.00	$110.00	$10.00
B	$110.00	$120.00	$10.00
C	$120.00	$130.00	$10.00
D	$130.00	$0.00	$0.00
Totals	$460.00	$360.00	$30.00

In this example, Investor A, B and C all made money (after fees and commissions), and Investor D is left with –$130. Investors as a whole show a balance of –$100 less expenses.

Example 2: Investor A purchased a share of stock from a company for $100

Out of pocket money..*In pocket money*
- Investor A $100.....................sells to Investor B for $90
- Investor B $90 ....sells to Investor C for $80
- Investor C $80......................sells to Investor D for $70
- Investor D $70

Total out of pocket..$–340
Total in-pocket $240
Total out of pocket.. –$100

In this example, all investors have lost money. Investor D's profit is –$70. Investors as a whole show a balance of –$100 less expenses.

Example 3: Investor A purchased a share of stock from a company for $100

Out of pocket money...*In pocket money*
- Investor A $100..................sells to Investor B for $100
- Investor B $100 ....sells to Investor C for $100
- Investor C $100..................sells to Investor D for $100
- Investor D $100

Total out of pocket..$–400

Total in-pocket $300

Total out of pocket .... –$100

In this example, all four investors lost money once you take out fees and commissions. The broker would avoid showing you this, but if he did, he would claim this is what they call a zero-sum gain. But in fact, you're playing a minus-sum game. In the end the company got the money, but Investor D is $100 in the hole and will be until he finds a buyer for his shares. Investors as a whole are down $100 + expenses.

Example 4: Investor A purchased a share of stock from a company for $100

Out of pocket money...*In pocket money*
- Investor A $100..................sells to Investor B for $90
- Investor B $90 ....sells to Investor C for $100
- Investor C $100..................sells to Investor D for $90
- Investor D $90

Total out of pocket..$–380

Total in-pocket $280

Total out of pocket .... –$100

In this example, Investor B makes $10, but Investors A, C and D are minus $110 (plus added fees and commissions). When the broker explains this, he would show that Investor B made $10, and Investor D has a $90 value. Investors as a whole are out $100 + expenses.

Remember, if one investor makes money, it's at the expense of one or more other investors. And, as I've explained, when you factor in fees, commissions and taxes, the transaction becomes a minus-sum game for investors. The more you play, the worse it gets.

You can't beat the system, because the system itself is designed against you. And yes, 5 percent will make money. Some will even make a lot of money. But the winners who make the 5 percent are paid by the other 95 percent of investors. Ask yourself who those people are that are losing money so that the investor makes money. Is it a rich guy in a mansion who doesn't care if he's losing money? No, in this day and age, it's likely your 401 (k) or pension plan that is losing money. The only sure thing about trying different ways to beat the system is the motion takes money out of the pockets of investors and puts it into the pockets of a select few.

You have been taught to believe that with a book, newsletter, seminar, or financial advisor, you can beat the system and be a financial winner. The thing you need to recognize about these sales pitches is that they are constructed in a rhythmic pattern. Each leads you through an explanation of the markets and then sell you on why that specific system is the best one to win money. You are treated to examples of people who have successfully used the system, charts that highlight how the system works, and a plea that you act now to avoid being left out of this "sure thing." What they leave out is complete statistics, the stories of those who lost money, and any true statements that they have no more knowledge of the markets than anyone else.

The people who produce and promote these programs have, in essence, figured out the only way to beat the system: They get you to buy their program and create a consistent flow of money into their pockets that the markets cannot provide. In return, these programs advance the perception that the system can be beaten and that they are designed in the best interest of the investors. As long as everyone is playing by the rules, the programs' designers don't feel unethical in taking advantage of the con to put your money in their pockets. But they know you can't beat the system.

Why good information told to too many people becomes bad information

Let's say you went to a poker game knowing that the cards were marked. What do you do? Well, you could use that information to your advantage, and as long as you didn't tell anyone, that is good information. It's not ethical and I don't recommend it, but it's part of my overall point. Now, if you told everyone that the cards were marked, then the game goes back to an equal playing ground, and the truth is no longer valuable information.

It's the same way with the stock market in predicting the movement of stocks. Its possible one guy could beat the system for a while, but as soon as other investors find out and start following suit, his method loses its value. Think of that the next time you see a book on how to beat the markets.

If you magically knew the final scores of the National Football League games for the upcoming week before they happened, would you go on TV and tell everyone you could, or would you use that information for yourself? The fact is that Vegas would pull the games off the board to avoid losing hundreds of millions to bettors, including you. Your good information has now become bad information.

As the old saying goes, "If three people can keep a secret, it's because two of them are dead." Consequently, if there were some magic formula to beat the markets, a few people could only benefit from it for a short period of time. No matter how good it is, when the masses find out about it, it's back to an equal playing field—and a minus-sum game.

You can never produce more winners than losers; it's impossible. You can't beat the system. A few do, but it helps to have inside information, participate in some type of illegal (or ethically questionable) market manipulation, or have special advantages such as having a seat on the exchange. The only sure winners are the brokers and exchanges who generate fees and commissions. So Wall Street firms train their brokers to keep a relentless focus on the eagle's eye view to keep investors rooted in the game.

If you think you can beat the system because you believe the markets are regulated and overseen by commissions that ensure fair play among all, consider this: the markets are all self-regulated. That means that the fox has been put in charge of the hen house. These regulatory agencies exist to establish and enforce rules merely to ensure fair play. They are concerned not with protecting the investors from the organizations but with protecting organizations from the investors. And, more important, just because there are a lot of rules doesn't mean there are a lot of *good* rules.

Any way you look at it, the true role of regulatory commissions for the stock market and commodity markets is to

- ensure the exchanges are successful;
- ensure the winners get their money;
- ensure the losers can't hold the brokers or exchanges liable; and
- ensure the brokers and exchanges are not required to keep any records negative to their success.

It's up to the regulatory commissions to keep the markets functioning, because the markets don't survive because investors are making money. They survive because investors are losing money. Winners in the markets attract the losers, and the markets survive on the losing investors. But the markets don't want to promote the fact that they need losing investors to survive. And without new blood, the system would collapse.

Plus, consider that without the markets, the regulators would be without a job because they have nothing to regulate. This may not affect the head of the Securities and Exchange Commission, but it certainly would affect their approximately 3,500 employees. And that's just one regulatory commission.

This is the reason the exchanges and brokerage firms do not keep or release any meaningful statistics that track investors' money. If the public had access to this information, we would see that it is impossible to beat the system, and we would see the vast amounts of money that is funneled every day from the pockets of investors into the pockets of Wall Street.

Bottom line: You can't beat the system. (Got it?)

2
The Hidden Truth—It's All Gambling

Whatever your thoughts on Bill O'Reilly, he was on the mark when he said that Las Vegas had moved their operations to lower Manhattan. The stock and commodity markets are gambling facilities, nothing more and nothing less. It's difficult to wrap our minds around the fact that what you think is investing is in fact straight gambling. The truth is that Wall Street, the mercantile exchanges, and others are all gambling facilities as much as any casino in Las Vegas. They all operate under self-regulated rules, but the difference is that exchanges have to market themselves to the public as something they are not so they can draw a continuous line of new investors.

Several years ago, Vanguard founder Jack Bogle said Wall Street was a casino croupier skimming a third right off the top of the market returns. They own the casino, fix the

odds, control the tables. Capitalism and investing requires an understanding between the public and the financial community that everything is legit and the games are not rigged. Do you really believe that Wall Street is honest with mainstream America? But you still give your money to them, and you still gamble.

Why do you gamble?

- You like predicting the unpredictable.
- You like to make a lot of money with a little money with no effort.
- You like to win.
- You think it's your only hope to ever accumulate financial security.
- It proves to others that you are willing to take a risk.
- It proves you are right, know what you are talking about, and are willing to put something of value at risk to prove it.
- You like to beat the odds.
- You like bragging rights, superiority, self-esteem.
- You gamble to lose to increase the euphoria of winning.
- You, unfortunately, need to feed an addiction.
- The psychology makes it harder to walk away.

Here's the thing: Casinos are promoted as pure entertainment, with no reason to promote themselves as something other than what they are. The markets, however, are promoted as performing an important business function with a vital economic value. In a casino, you are playing games marketed as a fun activity. No value attaches to the games themselves. You know that you are gambling, and the name of the game is insignificant. A poker game is a poker game. Roulette, craps, blackjack . . . they're just games. They have no vital economic importance to society.

Las Vegas never denies that the casinos are primarily gambling facilities. Even with the best restaurants, star-studded shows, and luxurious amenities, you know upfront these are available to enhance the gambling environment to bring your money into the specific casino. You may enjoy these activities, but try as you might, you can't hide the fact that you are at a casino to gamble.

To camouflage the market's reality—that it's a huge gambling casino—Wall Street managers needed to convince the public that people were actually investing to enhance their savings and promote the economy of the United States. This is a formidable task. Wall Street had to circumvent all of the entertainment and amenities that casinos offer and change your mindset to get you to believe that the stock market and commodity markets are a business function vital to everyone's well being. You trust that you're investing because you've been convinced the games are actually a legitimate financial venture.

To get you to believe you're investing, the exchanges had to attach something of value to the names of the games. They took symbols that we believed were vital to our economy and used them as titles on their games (stock names, commodities, etc.). This allowed them to seduce the public into thinking they were investing in something of substance. In reality, they'd merely changed the title of the games, but it's still the same gambling games that you find in Las Vegas. Either way, the key thing to remember is that the main element of all the games is that players or investors are trying to predict an unpredictable. And the odds are stacked in favor of the house.

A major difference between gambling at a casino and gambling in the markets is that the markets present advantages to an elite few that the average investor doesn't have. In a casino, you may be treated as a high roller, with VIP treatment and access to parts of the casino that average people will never see. But at the end of the day, the games you choose to play for a high buy-in are the same games average people are playing on the main floor. On Wall Street, an elite few have access to inside information, a seat on the exchange, the ability to act on information instantly as opposed to when it hits the public, and access to information that the public doesn't receive. Some of this is legal, some not. All of these advantages result in an increase in the odds in favor of a select few, to the detriment of average investors.

There is a strong natural tendency for you as an investor to ignore your losses and focus on your winnings. Casinos encourage this tendency by making sure that every quarter won in a slot machine causes lights to flash and makes its own little jingle in the metal tray. Seeing all the lights and hearing all the clinking, it's not hard to get the impression that everyone's winning. If you watch the floor of the New York Stock Exchange, with all of the yelling and running around and the flashing lights and the stock ticker, one cannot help but be caught up in the excitement thinking that fortunes are being made on the floor.

But losses are mostly silent.

So, while casinos are up front on the fact that they are gambling facilities, Wall Street camouflages its motives through manipulation, conditioning and relentless marketing to convince you that you are investing, trading, hedging, or speculating . . . anything else but gambling. Traders take advantage of the fact that you are searching for security to build a solid financial future for your family and your country.

In Las Vegas, gamblers are told the odds in advance, and even the most novice player understands that if you gamble long enough, the house will win. In the markets, you are not told the odds, only that there is some risk involved. This risk is sugar-coated by the allure of winning by following the newest system.

The stock market convinces you that investing in companies is a manageable risk, when you are actually gambling against other investors to get your money back. In the commodities market, you are told you are participating in a program that helps determine market prices, when in fact you are gambling, trying to outguess other investors to make money on the contract you purchased. The key factor they all have in common is that they serve the primary goal of Wall Street to keep your money in motion while creating no products or services in return.

Let me ask you a question: Why do Las Vegas bookmakers create the betting lines for a football game? It's not to predict an accurate outcome for the selected game (or there wouldn't be the 1/2 in the lines), but simply to get gamblers to bet equally on both teams. This is also why betting lines are adjusted from the point the betting line is established until right before the game starts. Bookmakers will adjust the line to increase the bets on one side or the other to balance them out. This ensures that despite the payout, the bookmakers and casinos win every time.

As a comparison, the betting lines, stock market, and commodity market prices are all affected by outside and unpredictable forces, whether it is the earnings report for a company, the weather forecast for a commodity, or an injury report for a football game.

In fact, if you line up Wall Street, the commodity markets, and casinos side by side for comparison, you'll see that they have nine things in common (see table on pages 33–35).

Wall Street has learned to take advantage of your search for security. As a group, people are willing to ignore logic and facts for a chance to gain financial security. If you think about it, isn't that the whole motivation around the lottery?

I've personally never seen a millionaire scratching off a lottery ticket, but I've seen plenty of poor folks struggling to make ends meet throw their money away for a nearly impossible chance at financial security.

Wall Street knows that when you are considering participating in a 401 (k) or pension plan, you are seeking a way to ensure financial security for you and your family. They use that in their marketing campaign and sales pitch. It's easy for brokers to pull you into the web when you want to believe what they have to sell. It's easy for them because you don't want to believe you're gambling. You want to believe in sure things. So you give over your money hoping the broker's promise of a "sure thing" will turn out to be a certainty. But since you're involved in predicting an unpredictable, there is no "sure thing."

Brokers are salesmen first and foremost. They are trained to sell you stocks, bonds, commodities, whatever gambling game you want to play to get your money in motion. They're taught to convince you to downplay the risk and follow their advice to win money in the markets. Of course it's a gamble, they'll say, but by (fill in the blank), you will make money. Of course they talk about the risks, but only as an example of investors who listened to bad advice or (even worse) tried to play the markets on their own.

The key is that Vegas and the markets constantly need to attract new gamblers to stay in business. If you look at it in any logical way, all three produce a much greater percentage of losers to winners, and the losers are what fuel the system. In trying to outsmart the system, we are drawn into the system, and the system itself is designed to create financial losers to survive.

Either way, the fact is that investors are gambling in a minus-sum game against fellow investors by trying to predict an unpredictable for financial gain. It's OK to gamble as long as you know the odds and risks going in. The fact that the stock market and the commodity markets don't tell you the odds makes it easy to conclude that casinos are the most legitimate of the three.

The nine elements that casinos, Wall Street and the commodities market have in common			
Element	Casinos	Stock Market	Commodity Markets
From simple to complex games	Slot machines to baccarat and horse racing, spending hours studying trends and charts	Simple stock purchase to those who spend hours/day studying the myriad of information/charts/graphs in order to make an educated guess.	Simple contracts to studying complex formulas affecting the circumstances of the contract
Ways to separate investors from their money	*Gamblers* trade their money for chips	*Investors* trade their money for shares	*Investors* trade their money for contracts
Need to guarantee investors get their money	Casinos guarantee they will buy *gamblers* chips back for the agreed value of the chips	If investors sell their shares, the Exchange will make sure they get their money.	Exchanges collect the money up front in the form of 'margin money' and pay the winners from this fund.
Losing is the foreplay of winning.	*Gamblers* play games, losing more than they win, but hoping to win big. *Gamblers* have to lose in order to get the thrill out of winning.	*Investors* buy and sell stocks, losing more than they win, but hoping to win big. *Investors* have to lose in order to get the thrill out of winning.	*Investors* buy and sell contracts, losing more than they win, but hoping to win big. *Investors* have to lose in order to get the thrill out of winning.

continued on next page

The nine elements that casinos, Wall Street and the commodities market have in common			
Element	Casinos	Stock Market	Commodity Markets
Investors do not like to place their money down once and walk away.	*Gamblers* like to stay in the game. The games are all designed to play over and over again. The system is set up to buy and sell by the second.	*Investors* like to stay in the game. The games are all designed to play over and over again. The system is set up to buy and sell by the second.	*Investors* like to stay in the game. The games are all designed to play over and over again. The system is set up to buy and sell by the second.
Investors risk something of value in a game.	*Gamblers* trade money for chips.	*Investors* trade money for shares.	*Investors* trade money for a commodities contract.
A self-regulatory system in place	Gambling commissions for each state that allows legalized gambling (example: Nevada Gaming Commission, NGC)	Security and Exchange Commission (SEC)	National Futures Association (NFA), tthe Commodity Futures Trading Commission (CFTA) & others.
Have no legal recourse if investors lose their money	All encouragement to participate in their games is followed by disclaimers that say that *gamblers* are responsible for their losses, based on rules written by the regulatory commissions.	All encouragement to participate in their games is followed by disclaimers that say that *investors* are responsible for their losses, based on rules written by the regulatory commissions.	All encouragement to participate in their games is followed by disclaimers that say that *investors* are responsible for their losses, based on rules written by the regulatory commissions.

The nine elements that casinos, Wall Street and the commodities market have in common			
Element	Casinos	Stock Market	Commodity Markets
Not required to keep records that will be a negative to the organizations	Casinos are not required to keep records that state how many *players* lost money or how much.	Exchanges are not required to keep records on how the *investors'* money is divided. The brokers are not required to keep performance records.	Exchanges are not required to keep records on how the *investors'* money is divided. The brokers are not required to keep performance records.

3
The Hidden Truth about Motion

"For investors as a whole,
returns decrease as motion increases."
—Warren Buffet's Fourth Law of Motion (2005)

What is motion in relation to the markets, and why is it important? Every time you as an investor purchase a share of stock, make changes in a mutual fund, or fail to make changes in your fund, or buy and sell commodity contracts, motion is created. Each time motion occurs, brokers and exchanges collect a cut. If a broker wants to make a large commission, he needs to generate as much motion as possible. The more motion created, the more successful the exchanges are. You'll notice that there is no mention of your success with your investments playing into this equation.

Brokers and exchanges do not care if your investments are successful or not, only that you keep investing.

It's the motion that takes investing from a zero-sum gain to a minus-sum game. Brokers' and exchanges' main goal is to get your money as an investor into motion and keep it in motion. It's important that you remember this. Each time you initiate activity in the markets, motion is created, and fees and commissions are produced. And this motion takes money from your pockets and puts money in the pockets of a select few on Wall Street. And remember by Wall Street,

I'm referring to the financial services world, not a geographic location.

Once you enter their game, every time you buy and sell stocks or commodities, you are just shuffling money and paper among investors. Each transaction costs you real money in fees and commissions to brokers and exchanges. That produces a negative cash flow. In return, you get a piece of paper with so-called *published value*. This provides a false sense of security since published value is the greatest illusion of actual wealth. What you actually are doing is transferring real cash in exchange for pretend money.

Now you may believe that fees and commissions are the price of doing business and should not count into the bottom line that shows whether you make money or lose money, but look at this as a large spinning wheel. Every time the wheel turns, a penny falls off. The more turns, the more pennies fall off into the pockets of Wall Street. Doesn't sound like much until you realize the wheel turns millions of times every day the markets are open.

Therefore, the markets need that wheel spinning constantly to stay in business.

What keeps the wheel spinning?

1. Constantly changing prices without using a solid mathematical or scientific formula.
2. The ability to buy and sell by the second which creates volatility in the markets.

3. The volatility creates insecurity, which draws you back into the system by enticing investors to act.
4. This action accelerates motion.
5. The need to constantly find new investors or new blood.

Wall Street recognizes our need for security and designs its entire marketing campaign around providing a stable financial future that is almost cruel in its deception. Its managers created a process that takes advantage of investors' insecurity by creating volatility, which accelerates motion, which encourages investors to buy and sell to prevent being caught in a losing position. Fighting to gain or regain financial security likely puts investors further in debt. This plays right into their hands.

Unfortunately, when Wall Street firms get caught up in the same volatility, they immediately run to their cronies in Congress to bail them out. This encourages them to continue their deceptive practices because there are no real consequences. Try running up a huge credit card debt and then contact your congressman to see if you can get a bailout.

We know Wall Street has designed and developed this system, and it needs the brokers to find new investors and keep losing investors from leaving the market. You are their target, and they have to convince you that they are working on your behalf. They need to create a unique level of trust that permits you to hand over your money to them without question.

Without investors creating the motion, the markets would fail. The brokers and exchanges would go out of business.

What a process! Wall Street has created a whirlwind of confusion and motion to separate its clients from trillions of dollars of cash over the years and into its operators' own pockets. All this in return for issuing pieces of paper with no actual value, and yet members of the public believe they're rich.

What draws investors to the game of the markets?

Investors are pulled into the game by the opportunity of taking a little money and turning it into a lot of money quickly, without effort. This is done by constantly changing prices and buying and selling by the second, which are the main components of the stock market and commodities market.

There are those who buy into the dream that they can manipulate the markets to win big. For example: This is a simple formula for how an investor can use the pyramid of wealth formula to quickly turn his or her money once it is invested in the market:

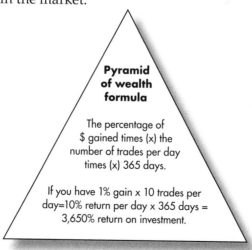

Pyramid of wealth formula

The percentage of $ gained times (x) the number of trades per day times (x) 365 days.

If you have 1% gain x 10 trades per day=10% return per day x 365 days = 3,650% return on investment.

The significance of the formula is that on a Certificate of Deposit, or bonds you would purchase at a bank, the rate of return is 5 percent a year. In the markets, investors have the possibility of making a 10 percent return in a day, multiplied by 365 days. The returns could be monumental if everything worked.

Margins in the commodity markets

In the commodity markets, margin money is used as an added incentive for investors to take a risk. A margin is like a down payment, by requiring investors to put down only a portion of the true value of the contract as risk, which averages out to approximately one-twentieth of the true value.

Putting up one-twentieth of the value of a commodity allows investors the possibility to make a twenty-fold return on its true value. This incentive allows investors to believe they can turn a little money into a lot of money quickly, without effort.

Now, I'll show you the same pyramid of wealth formula using margin money:

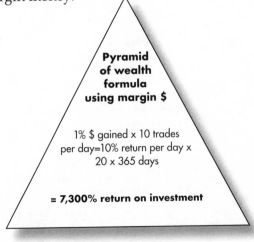

**Pyramid
of wealth
formula
using margin $**

1% $ gained x 10 trades
per day=10% return per day x
20 x 365 days

= 7,300% return on investment

Margin call: When the margin posted in the margin account is below the minimum margin requirement, the broker or exchange issues a call for more money to be put into the account. The investor now either has to increase the margin money that he has deposited or settle his contract.

With margins, investors are in the position of risking only one-twentieth of the amount to make a possible 7,300 percent return on investment, if they are making a 10 percent return in a day, multiplied by 365 days. The returns could be monumental, if everything worked in favor of the investor. The losses, which are a greater probability, can be devastating.

Margins also make it possible to sell a commodities contract you purchased and buy back more than you sold with the same money. For example, if a corn contract is $2.00 and margins required are one-twentieth, you pay ten cents in margin money to buy a bushel of corn ($2.00 divided by 20 = 10 cents). If corn goes up 10 cents, you can sell it for 20 cents, and take the 20 cents and buy two bushels of corn for the initial investment of 10 cents.

The obvious downfall is that you could make an incorrect prediction, or the exchange could ask you to contribute more money (known as a "margin call") and you could be in serious financial difficulty. Margins should be eliminated in the commodity markets, period. If an investor wants to take a risk on a contract, they should be required to put up all of the risk.

The power of "doubling up"

Despite the obvious risks, it's this mental process of doubling up on winnings that brings investors into the game.

To show you the power of doubling up, let's use the "child's birthday" scenario. Let's say you put one dollar into your child's savings account on her first birthday, and you doubled it to two dollars on her second birthday and four on her third birthday, and so on, this is what would happen by the time your child was twenty-one years old:

Contribute $1 at age 1	Age 2 $2	Age 3 $4
Age 4 $8	Age 5 $16	Age 6 $32
Age 7 $64	Age 8 $128	Age 9 $256
Age 10 $512	Age 11 $1024	Age 12 $2048
Age 13 $4096	Age 14 $8192	Age 15 $16,384
Age 16 $32,768	Age 17 $65,536	Age 18 $131,072
Age 19 $262,144	Age 20 $524,288	Age 21 $1,048,576

Now, imagine if you can use margin money to do this over the course of several hours, days or weeks instead of years. This is a great deal as long as prices work in your favor. But there are no guarantees or formulas either way. It's this appeal of almost instant wealth that draws investors into the game and creates the motion. And this motion takes money out of the pockets of investors and puts money into the pockets of a select few on Wall Street. This greed and unpredictability leads to the eventual downfall of the investors, because as I observed earlier, the wins can be substantial, the losses devastating.

The only constant in keeping investors' money in motion is that the prices continually change, brokers collect their commissions, exchanges collect their fees, and the government collects taxes on any gains. Remember that the sole purpose of Wall Street is to keep your money in constant motion, and keeping it in motion results in a minus-sum game for investors as a whole.

Now, this is a brilliant strategy of Wall Street, thanks to the fees and commissions produced with each motion generated. If you play long enough, Wall Street will wind up with all of your money in time, with no real accountability for where it goes.

4

The Hidden Truth about Published Value, Perceived Value and Outperformed

If you have a share of stock with published value, you have no money, with no promise of real money to back it up. We're living in a world where we are relying increasingly on paper with published value with no promise to pay and with no money to back it up! Millions of times a day, investors in the markets trade real money in return for a piece of paper to use to gamble with other investors. All you've done is pay a cover charge to play the game. The person holding the paper has no real money until someone decides to buy your paper. More important, the paper has no real value outside of the markets.

Look what has happened in the real estate market in 2008. Millions of homeowners trying to sell their houses have found out that their homes are worth only the price a buyer is willing to pay. At least homes have some sort of

tangible value. If you had to, you could sell materials from your house, rent out your house, or otherwise find a way to produce something of value out of the land. The same cannot be said for shares of stock.

Here's what you need to know about published value:

- Shares of stock are as valuable as the piece of paper their printed on;
- the guy holding the paper has no money and never will as long as he's holding the paper;

- the actual value of the share is ZERO;
- there is no money to back up the shares and no guarantee that you will find a buyer;
- unlike casino chips, there's no place to turn a share back in for money;
- until the share is removed from the exchange, there will always be someone holding the bag;
- 99 percent of all listed shares will eventually wind up in the dumpster; and
- the average life of a publicly traded company is eight years.

The price listed for the individual share is what is called "published value." When the share is issued from the company, the company keeps the money and gives you a piece of paper in return. The piece of paper is good only to trade among investors and generates money for the broker and exchanges until it is removed from trading. It has no real value; it's only based on the perception of the buyers and sellers. Until you sell your shares, you have nothing of value. It's like holding chips in Vegas at a casino that won't buy them back. Casino chips have value and shares do not. Ninety-nine percent of the paper you hold will wind up in the dumpster. It's up to you whether you are the one throwing it away.

You saw a small sample of this during the dot-com crash earlier this decade, which saw scores of people who were millionaires on paper one day, broke or millions of dollars in debt the next as the published value of their stock went in the toilet. The truth is they were broke on both days; it was only their published value that changed.

You're seeing it in 2008 as Wall Street firms are finding out the paper they are holding in subprime (junk) loans are worthless. They became worthless when mortgage owners walked away when they could no longer afford the payments. These firms flourished when they were making money hand-over-fist by giving out loans, but now are crying for a bailout when their scheme failed.

Let's revisit the example of how Wall Street uses published value and perceived value in the stock market:

Example 1: Investor A purchased a share of stock from a company for $100

        Out of pocket money...............................*In pocket money*
- Investor A $100.................. sells to Investor B for $110
- Investor B $110...................sells to Investor C for $120
- Investor C $120.................. sells to Investor D for $130
- Investor D $130

Total out of pocket..$460

Total in-pocket $360

Total out of pocket... −$100

In this example, Investor A, B and C all made money (after fees and commissions), and Investor D is −$130. Investors as a whole are −$100 + expenses.

Example 2: Investor A purchased a share of stock from a company for $100

Out of pocket money..................................*In pocket money*
- Investor A $100....................sells to Investor B for $90
- Investor B $90.....................sells to Investor C for $80
- Investor C $80....................sells to Investor D for $70
- Investor D $70

Total out of pocket... $340

Total in-pocket $240

Total out of pocket.. −$100

In this example, all investors have lost money. Investor D is −$70. Investors as a whole are −$100 + expenses.

Example 3: Investor A purchased a share of stock from a company for $100

Out of pocket money..................................*In pocket money*
- Investor A $100..................sells to Investor B for $100
- Investor B $100 ....sells to Investor C for $100
- Investor C $100..................sells to Investor D for $100
- Investor D $100

Total out of pocket... $400

Total in-pocket $300

Total out of pocket.. −$100

In this example, all four investors lost money once you take out fees and commissions. The broker would avoid showing you this, but if he did, he would claim this is a zero-sum gain, but in fact, it is a minus-sum game. The company got the money, and Investor D is out $100. Investors as a whole are out $100 + expenses.

Example 4: Investor A purchased a share of stock from a company for $100

 Out of pocket money..............................*In pocket money*
- Investor A $100.....................sells to Investor B for $90
- Investor B $90 ....sells to Investor C for $100
- Investor C $100...................sells to Investor D for $90
- Investor D $90
Total out of pocket..$380
Total in-pocket $280
Total out of pocket...................................−$100

In this example, Investor B makes $10, but Investor A, C and D are minus $110 (plus added fees and commissions). When the broker explains this, he would show that Investor B made $10, and Investor D has a $90 value. Investors as a whole are out $100 plus expenses.

Investor D represents the millions of investors in this country who hold approximately $15 trillion of published value stocks today. They have paper worth, but no cash money in pocket. And what will happen to all of the Investor Ds of the world? They will be replaced with Investor E, and so on. And that process continues to create motion. And eventually, the share will float among investors until it is removed from trading. When that happens, the last Investor (D, E or whoever) will be holding an empty bag.

The danger we're facing now is that millions of everyday Americans with retirement plans and pensions are in the same boat. One day their published and perceived value will be exposed as worthless pieces of paper, and I would like to prevent this from happening to you as it happened to me at Eastern Airlines.

If you learn nothing else from *The Losing Game*, I would like you to understand that the terms "published value," "perceived value" and "outperformed" are words of illusion with no real value. They give you a positive outlook on a negative situation, but nothing to sink your teeth into.

You see, unless you have actual cash in your pocket, what you have listed on a piece of paper is just that—a piece of paper. Published value is just an assigned value, and it has no real value until you find someone to give you money in return for the paper. Perceived value is just how valuable you think you are.

If you look at those three terms:

- They do not represent true value;
- brokers use these terms to deceive investors and avoid accountability; and
- hearing them can give investors a positive outlook on a negative situation.

Real value vs. published value or perceived value

If your broker told you that your portfolio had a published value of a million dollars and had outperformed the S&P 500, you would think you were a millionaire. Except the paper you hold cannot be turned into real money without a buyer. All you can do is move it from one investor to another. The paper you hold has an unpredictable selling price. Until you find a buyer, your pockets are as empty as they were that morning. Now, go to the grocery store and buy bread and milk with your published value.

You have perceived value that says you are a millionaire, but take some shares of stock to go to a fast-food restaurant and try to buy lunch. Or take a commodities contract to the bank and see if they'll give you a loan. What you hold in your hand is perceived value. You perceive you have money from the published value of the paper, but you can't trade that paper for anything of value.

The illusion Wall Street has created is perceived value, which is the money you imagine you can redeem for something, but does not exist. The deception is published value which is the value assigned by society. Both are illusions of actual wealth. You cannot go to the grocery store and buy food with your perceived or published value. The only way you as an investor can know your true wealth at the end of the day is the actual money you have in your pocket.

You've seen how perceived value and published value add up to a ticking time-bomb, and that cannot be overstated. As of this writing, there is approximately $300 trillion of outstanding derivative contracts, as well as approximately $16 trillion in published value of outstanding stock. This is an astonishing concept, because it's well beyond the amount of money that can be printed, spent or kept.

Consider this:

If you spent a million dollars a day, you would be well over *three thousand years old* before you spent a trillion dollars.

Let's look at this another way. Congress passes a $700 billion bailout they claim is an economic rescus package. However, here's what you could do with the $700 billion that's going to bailout the nation's financial industry, courtesy of *Time* magazine.

- You could give every person in the United States $2,300 or give every household $6,300.
- You could buy gas for every car in the United States for the next 16 months.
- You could pay the income taxes for every American who makes $500,000 or less.
- You could fully fund the departments of Defense, Treasury, Education, State, Veterans Affairs, Interior Department and NASA.
- You could buy every NFL, NBA, Major League Baseball team, build each one a new stadium and pay every player $191 million each for a year.
- You could pay off 7% of the nation's $9.8 trillion debt.

Bottom line is, the government can do a lot better than reward Wall Street firms that made consistently bad loans by purchasing their paper and hoping to dump it on someone else for a profit.

The reason is that the money to back that paper doesn't exist. It can't exist and won't ever exist in the future. It's a numbers game and a paper shuffle among investors. The simple fact is that Wall Street convinced you that having published value means real money is involved. But it's a lie. The money isn't there. The only money generated goes from your pocket to the pockets of the Wall Street money managers. They now have real money, and you have a piece of paper. Do you still think brokers are working in your best interests?

As we're learning, investors are being conned into participating in a minus-sum gambling game played with paper circulating among investors until the paper finally goes out of circulation. Eventually the motion will eat it up, or the paper will lose its value. And the hundreds of trillions of dollars in outstanding stock and commodities contracts create a vast wasteland of perceived value with no cash to back it up.

When a stock is issued, it is registered in a computer system with the name of the shareholder attached to it.

The only two ways you can remove an issued stock share:

1. The company buys it back (happens approximately 1 percent of the time);
2. The company or share is removed from trading.

Money is generated to investors as a whole only when the company buys back its shares, which happens about 1 percent of the time. It's not like taking your T-bill or Certificate of Deposit to the bank and the bank paying you the value of the paper. In that case, you've retired the paper. Now the difference is that companies retiring a share only happens about 1 percent of the time. The other 99 percent remains out there, shuffling between investors. Once again, there is no money there. It is a perceived value.

So, real money is separated from investors, without creating a product or service and transferred to a few parasitic money managers. This process increases the standard of living for these Wall Street parasites, who extract actual money from the transaction, and decreases the standard of living for the investors, whose real wealth is transformed into published wealth. This process results in a negative pull on the economy by taking disposable income from the public and funneling it to a select few on Wall Street. But, you have satisfied the goal of Wall Street by placing your money in motion. And by keeping that money in motion Wall Street continues to skim your money off the top, creating *nothing* in return.

Outperformed what (or who)?

The term *outperformed* is simple in its deception. You can have two investors who lost in the markets, and one outperformed the other. You can have two winners in the market, and one outperformed the other. If you don't know what you were performing against, and you don't include all the statistics, the word has absolutely no value.

Here are a few examples:

Example 1: Your broker is pushing you to buy shares in Company A because it outperformed market expectations for the last quarter. Now, Company A was expected to lose

$50 million and it only lost $45 million, so it outperformed expectations, even though it lost $45 million. Wall Street is happy, while investors, employees and consumers suffer.

Example 2: Company B claims it outperformed Company A, even though Company B loses $40 million. Sure, Company B outperformed Company A by 20 percent—they both lost money.

Example 3: A makes $1,000 and B makes $1,001. B outperformed A, but the gain is insignificant.

"Outperformed" can mean anything. In the absence of full disclosure and accountability, the broker can avoid giving you honest statistics. This kind of double-talk makes it appear that *outperformed* is an improvement over a negative, or an improvement over a positive. It makes a poor or negative situation look like a positive.

The brilliance of all of this rhetorical strategy is that investors are convinced to pay a "cover charge" of real money in return for an issued piece of paper that allows you to play Wall Street's game of chance. You are now among those who are out $15 trillion in case of economic collapse and who are part of a gigantic paper shuffling between investors. Look at the charts and see that there is no money created in the motion; it just puts investors, as a whole, deeper in debt.

Let's say I went to the investment department in my bank and had them draw me up an investment proposal. Now, what if I were to take that proposal to the loan department and see if they'll give me a loan based on that investment proposal? My banker would say they wouldn't give me a loan based on the recommendations of their investment department, and I'm one of their better customers. Preferred or not, I'm quite sure your banker would say the same thing.

When you review your financial reports, remember the terms "published value," "perceived value," and "outperformed," and see if they appear in your broker's vocabulary. If they do, you're in danger of being left holding the bag when it's time to collect your retirement or pension.

5
The Hidden Truth about the Stock Market

Here's a story that was told to me:

Once upon a time in a village, a man appeared and announced to the villagers that he would buy monkeys for $10 each. The villagers, seeing that there were many monkeys around, went out to the forest and started catching them.

The man bought thousands of monkeys at $10, and as the supply started to diminish, the villagers stopped catching them. The man then announced that he would now buy monkeys for $20. This renewed the efforts of the villagers, and they started catching monkeys again.

Soon, the supply diminished even further, and people started going back to their farms. The offer increased to $25 for each monkey, but the supplies of monkeys were so scarce that it was hard to even see a monkey, let alone catch one.

The man then announced that he would buy monkeys for $50! However, since he had to return to the city on some business, his assistant would now buy on his behalf.

In the man's absence, the assistant told the villagers, "Look at all of these monkeys in the big cage that the man has collected. I will sell them to you at $35 each, and when my boss returns from the city, you'll be able to sell them to him for $50 each."

The villagers rounded up all of their savings and bought all of the monkeys from the assistant.

They never saw the man or his assistant again, only monkeys everywhere they looked.

Now you have a better understanding of how the stock market works.

I'm trying to get you to quit turning your money over with blind confidence to a money manager you believe has your best interest at heart. To do this, I have to make you understand that what you've been trained to think the stock market is and what the reality is are two separate things.

From my discussions with average people, this is what they think the stock market is:

- They think the stock market is a legitimate place to invest your money.
- They think all publicly traded companies make a profit.
- They think that, if they invest in those companies, they will share in their growth and profit.

- They think that the people who handle their money are working in their best interests.
- They think they are securing their future through safe investing in a 401 (k), pension, or retirement fund, with minimal risk.
- They think the prices of shares are based on the financial report and performance of the company.
- They think that the system is so hard to understand, it's OK to hand over their money in confidence to brokers or money managers.

At that point, they walk away confidently thinking their retirement and investments are secure.

In fact, it's hard for most people to believe the stock market is simply a highly complex con game created, developed and controlled by Wall Street. To keep it operating, Wall Street's managers need to make sure the company, brokers, exchanges, and the government get their money. If you are making money with your 401 (k), retirement, or pension fund through the stock market, that means that others who may have the same retirement plans are losing money. In a minus-sum game, the system must have more financial losers than winners, since it's the losers that support the system.

When you invest, your participation in the markets consists of a piece of paper that has published value. It is a contract that protects Wall Street from you when you lose your money. It guarantees only that everyone involved plays by the rules. It holds no guarantees that you can find a buyer or that you will receive cash money in return for the buyer taking possession of your paper.

In most situations in which you purchase shares of stocks from a publicly traded company . . .

- the company receives free capital,
- the brokers and commissions make money through commissions and fees,
- the IRS makes money off of your winnings, and
- all investors as a whole lose money.

The system is set up by Wall Street to benefit the money managers at the expense of the investors. Since I described a good deal as one in which all parties benefit and investors as a whole lose money, the market is not a good deal for all.

This has resulted in a process in which most investors lose money, with the only sure winners being the companies, brokers, and exchanges. If you don't believe me, show me the numbers that will show how many investors make money and how many investors lose money in the markets. (I will save you some time: they don't exist.) And where does the money come from if you make money? Most of the time, it comes from other investors. We have been taught to ignore who these other investors are. I've had people tell me point-blank when I ask them where their winnings come from in the market: "I don't care."

The fact is you should care, because the other investors are your grandparents' savings, retirement funds, the pension of a widow, and investors who trust the wrong people with their life savings. This is what they don't tell you, what they don't want you to know. Ask around. See who is losing money, and tell me if they live in a mansion or across the street from you.

The reality of the stock market is you're not investing

Consider my definition of investing as "a 100 percent possibility of everyone making money based on the profit from the production of goods or services." Based on that definition, the reality is that from the beginning, you are not investing: you are gambling. You are entering in a minus-sum game in which, at the end of each day, investors as a whole have less money in pocket than they started with. You are participating in an unpredictable game, but the results are predictable . . . investors as a whole will lose money. You have satisfied the goal of Wall Street by putting your money in motion. The process of gambling has begun.

Let me walk you through this process: When a publicly traded company issues a share, the company receives your money in return for the share and does not pay it back. Let's follow the progression and do the math. You pay a fee to a broker, who then takes your money and buys a share from a company. The price you paid for paper and fees are nonrefundable, and the company is no longer involved. The company's name provides a reference point for selling the shares at a later date, but there is no mathematical or scientific formula to determine the price of shares. What's important to know is that the price of the shares is not determined by any formula or company financial report but strictly by the mental state of the investors. The buyer has to believe his money is worth less than your share, and you have to think his money is worth more than your paper. No matter how valuable you believe your share to be, unless you find someone to purchase it, the price is completely negotiable.

The process of buying stocks

- Investor A gives money to a broker.
- Broker charges fee and gets commission for trade.
- Broker gives money to exchange.
- Exchange gets a fee.
- Exchange then issues a share.
- The company gets the money, which they don't pay back.
- Exchange has your share with your name on it.
- There is no guarantee you can sell your share, no guaranteed price. The share has a non-predictable selling price.
- If Investor A wants their money back, they have to pay a broker to sell the share to Investor B.
- The broker collects fees and commissions. The price Investor B pays is based totally on what the buyer is willing to pay. There's no way to rationalize the price, it's all subjective.
- Investor B will sell to Investor C, Investor C sells to Investor D, and so on . . .

- Each movement involves fees and commissions paid to the brokers and exchanges. This process will continue until the shares are removed from the exchange
- The last investor is holding an empty bag
- The last investor has no real money, and there is no money to retire the stock
- The moment the share is purchased, you have now bought something with a non-predictable selling price.

Back to the math: You have purchased the right to put your name on a piece of paper (share) which is turned over to the exchange for a fee to be put into motion. Every time that paper is in motion, this takes money out of the pockets of investors and puts money in the pockets of the money managers. If you make money, that means one or more investors have to lose money. It's impossible for 100 percent of investors to make money. The last investor is left holding the bag, and there's no money to retire the stock. But he thinks he has real money. This is a good example of an investor having published value which is the greatest illusion of actual wealth. There is approximately $15 trillion of outstanding stock and no money with which to buy them back from investors. Investors think they are wealthy, but there's no money there.

When investors thinks they're investing, they're actually:

- trying to turn a little money into a lot of money quickly without effort;
- trying to predict an unpredictable;
- giving the exchanges and brokers a cut every time the shares are in motion;
- buying and selling shares based on the mental process of the investors, not on any mathematical or scientific formula; and
- not performing a business function but trying to out-predict other investors.

These are the classic definitions of gambling.

Make no mistake, the exchanges are gambling operations, and brokers are glorified bookies hustling investors from all sides to keep your money in motion so they can get their fees and commissions. Consequently, they do not care if you win money or lose money, only that your money remains in motion.

You've been taught to believe that all large companies are money-making ventures. You believe that investing in something of value can result in sharing equally in its growth and profit. As a result, as a company sees an increase in profits, you should see an equal return in proportion. Dividends are supposed to be paid to the shareholders for the use of their money. This does not happen. The fact is the company keeps the money up front when the stock is issued, and if one investor makes money, it comes out of the pocket of another investor. The company now has "free capital" to work with and is not obligated in any way to repay the investor.

If a publicly traded company pays a dividend at all, it is usually after it decides to reinvest the profit back into the company (called "retained earnings"). This happens at the discretion of the board of directors. If you factor in the money that goes to the company, likely not to be returned, along with fees and commissions for each transaction, you are participating in a minus-sum game. Remember, the published value is determined by the perception of the buyer, not on any proven scientific or mathematical formula.

Let's look at Microsoft as an example. For seventeen years, Microsoft had not paid dividends, funneling the money back into the company. By early 2004, Microsoft's cash balance had crossed $50 billion. In part, due to increasing pressure from shareholders, in 2003 the company declared its first ever dividend for common stock. Despite the reports that they were "rewarding" their stockholders, in fact, it's possible that they were merely trying to avoid a 39.5 percent corporate tax rate under an obscure rule that taxes companies that makes excessive profits.

Reality: A company does not share its profits equally with investors, and the average dividend they pay out is usually less than 1 percent.

If the company chooses not to pay dividends on the shares you have purchased, you have no chance of getting your original investment back from the company (only from selling the shares to another investor). And even if you receive a 2 percent dividend return (the average is 1 to 3 percent), it would take fifty years to get your original investment back. Even the chances of this happening are very remote, because the average life span of a publicly traded company is only eight years.

The key is you are entering a minus-sum game. From the very beginning investors pay their brokers a fee to give their money to a company in exchange for issued shares of stocks. That is one negative cash flow. The company doesn't pay back what the investor put in. That's a negative cash flow. The IRS taxes all investors' winnings as capital gains. That's a negative cash flow.

If one investor makes money off another investor, the IRS taxes all your winnings, the exchanges collect their fees, and the brokers collect their commissions.

Reality: The stock market is not required to keep records tracking where investors' money goes.

Here's an example:

An investor buys shares of stock for $100,000 and sells them to another investor for $200,000.

He makes $100,000 profit, minus fees and commissions.

Let's say for the sake of argument that he owes the IRS a capital gains tax of 35 percent, or $35,000, plus the exchange fees.

He decides to purchase another $200,000 worth of stock, but the company in which he invests goes broke, causing the investor to lose all $200,000.

He is allowed to write off only $3,000 that year against his losses.

He lost all of his money he had in the markets but still owes the government $32,000 in taxes for money he no longer has.

Either way, this creates a positive cash flow to the government, exchanges and brokers, and a minus-sum game to investors as a whole, no matter if you as an investor win or lose.

However, if you lose money, the exchanges still get their fees.

As an investor, the only positive cash flow you can have is through

1. The company buying back the stock (which happens on average about one percent of the time), or
2. the company paying a dividend (some companies don't pay a dividend, and the ones that do pay an average of 1 to 3 percent).

The federal government has allowed the financial crisis of 2008 to occur by failing to hold Wall Street accountable for investors' money and let them regulate themselves. In a free-market system, there should be a trust between business and the public that business should be able to regulate themselves, but instead they have colluded to keep outsiders in the dark. Can we afford to let Wall Street continue to make their own rules and keep the rest of us in the dark?

First of all, there's no real accountability to the system without full disclosure tracking investors' money. This has allowed us to be drawn into a minus-sum game in which we are shuffling paper with no real value among investors while Wall Street gets real money from the motion. And with the propaganda that is bombarded at the public daily, that's how investors get trapped into the system.

I have shown that you can't beat the system, because the stock market is a minus-sum gambling game for the investors from the moment they hand over their money to a company. The best advice I can give you is to quit losing money in the markets and invest it in yourself. How can it be bad for the economy? By taking your money out of the pockets of a select few and investing it in yourself and your community, it would be a positive to all but a few bitter Wall Street power brokers.

Why? They'll have to get a REAL job!

6
The Hidden Truth about the Commodities Market

M ost of us had a limited knowledge of the commodities market until the summer of 2008. When gas prices rose to over $150 per barrel for the first time ever, the public became interested in why this occurred. Debates over the role of speculators in the oil market and the effect of supply and demand were hotly debated but rarely explained. In fact, many of the products you purchase on a daily basis have their prices determined by actions in the commodity markets. Commodity markets control prices of not only oil, but corn, grain, soybeans, wheat, steel, and other basics listed. Even if you are not involved in the commodity markets, you need to understand how they affect your everyday life and how they take money out of your pockets and put money into the pockets of brokers and the exchanges.

The commodity markets are very complex in design. To describe the primary function of the commodity markets as they promote it in a few words is impossible. This is by design. No businessman would sign off on a program he doesn't understand. With the commodities market, if you can't understand it, you can't criticize it or regulate it. It's a system they need to get rid of.

Here are the basics as they stand today: The exchanges tell you the commodity markets offer a vital economic function by providing an effective and efficient mechanism for the management of price risks. They also assert that competitive price discovery has a main economic role and is a key economic benefit of futures trading. The commodities markets have been popularized as a measure of supply and demand, as a vehicle for keeping prices low, always working in the consumers' best economic interests. It's not true.

If you don't understand that, that's fine; it's a deception anyway. Here's all you need to know:

- The commodity markets are pure gambling.
- The goal of the investor purchasing a contract is to sell it to make money. But from the beginning, he is entering a minus-sum game. Remember, a minus-sum game means that at the end of the day, all investors have less money than they started with. They are stuck with exchange fees, broker commissions and taxes.

Here's how it works: You pay a fee to a broker, who then takes your margin money and gives it to the exchange, and buys a contract with a specified delivery or settlement date (the end of the contract). The published price you paid for the contract was not determined by any mathematical or scientific formula. The process for establishing contract prices is based on the mental process of the investors that involves an infinite number of factors. You've now purchased a contract with an unpredictable selling price. The process of gambling has begun.

To reconcile your contract, you have to pay a broker to sell or settle your contract on or before the settlement.

Reality: You are entering into a game of chance called gambling.

Margin money: down payment the holder of a contract uses to cover the risk.

The process of buying commodity contracts

- Investor A gives margin money to a broker to purchase a commodities contract.
- The broker charges a fee and gets commission for contract.
- The broker gives margin money to exchange.
- The exchange gets a fee, and the margin money is to cover losses if they occur.
- The exchange then issues a contract with a settlement date.
- There is no guarantee you can sell your contact and no guaranteed price. The contract has an unpredictable selling price.

Investor A is now in a high-risk situation, because from the moment he purchased the contract, the prices constantly change. If Investor A wants to settle the contract, he has to pay a broker to sell or settle the contract on or before the settlement date.

The broker collects fees and commissions on the settlement. The price of settlement is based totally on what the buyer is willing to pay. There's no way to rationalize the price. It's all subjective. If the prices change enough opposite his position, Investor A could lose his margin money, and if the prices keep changing, the exchange could call for more margin money to cover losses.

Remember, the brokers and exchanges don't care if you as an investor made money or lost money on the contract, because they always make money from the motion created by the contract. And it's this motion that takes money out of your pockets and puts it in the pockets of Wall Street.

When Investor A settles the contract, if he made money, it came from the other investors' margin money. If Investor A lost money, it goes from his margin money into the account of the other investor, minus fees and commissions.

Let's review the process of purchasing commodities:

- Investors are betting against each other trying to predict an unpredictable.
- The house (commodities exchange) gets a cut on every transaction.
- The odds are stacked against the investors.
- Investors are participating in a minus-sum game.
- Investors margin money is held in escrow to guarantee the winners get their money.
- Investors as a whole can't beat the system.

Slot machines, roulette wheels, and craps are all games of chance risking something of value in an attempt to predict the unpredictable. By playing the commodities market, you are playing similar games, except the names going around the wheel are familiar ones like corn and crude oil. Other games are named after absurd concepts such as degree days or cell phone minutes. The titles of the games are insignificant, as long as they draw investors to the games. Buying and selling contracts in the commodity markets are no different from feeding coins into slot machines.

Each contract purchased is just another pull of the lever, with the house always taking a cut. Investors do not share wealth from the production of these commodities, but simply participate in gambling games against other investors.

Once again, this is gambling, no more or no less.

Wall Street makes it complex and the brokers market it to us through these strategies:

- the use of weak and misleading words;
- the manipulation of and/or lack of statistics;
- changing the label of gambling to speculating, hedging, trading and investing;
- the vast amounts of types of contracts that can be written and the multitude of ways they can be executed;
- convincing us that the market provides economic value to consumers;
- convincing us that prices are discovered or reflected, not created;
- creating new games to generate additional revenue streams;

- creating a problem that didn't exist (volatility); and
- creating hedging to solve the problem (volatility) they created.

Don't count on the regulatory commissions to protect you as an investor. As I discussed earlier, the job of a self-regulatory organization is to enforce minimum financial sales practice requirements for its members. Nowhere does it mention the investor.

The true purposes of the regulatory agencies are to:

- ensure the exchanges are successful,
- ensure the winners get their money,
- ensure the losers can't hold the brokers or exchanges liable, and
- ensure the brokers and exchanges are not required to keep any records negative to their success.

I want to show you that if you study the commodity markets, they will tell you everything you need to know.

As one of the three regulatory agencies of the commodity market, (the other two being the Commodities Futures Trading Commission [CFTC] and the Futures Commissions Merchants [FCM]), the National Futures Association (NFA) regulates every firm or individual who conducts futures trading business with public customers. If you contact the NFA and tell them you are interested in the commodities market, they will send you a booklet, entitled "Opportunities and Risk: An Educational Guide to Trading Futures and Options

on Futures." The booklet will tell you this about the commodities market:

- It's very risky.
- It's very volatile.
- You should risk only capital *you can afford to lose.*
  [italics mine]

Brokers who successfully promote the commodities market are one part master salesman and one part con man. The
master salesman attracts your participation. From that point
on, he leads you to believe that if you play the game right,
using all his "expert" (but nonbinding) advice, you will win.
These are classic elements of a scam.

The booklet points out that success is based primarily
on an investor's emotional makeup; that many people are
not "mentally qualified to trade." If you follow the NFA's
advice and lose your money, you are prepared to accept their
escape: It wasn't their fault you lost your money. You weren't
"mentally qualified to trade."

"Opportunity and Risk"

I'm going to show you one example of how the NFA uses
illusion and deception to give you a false sense of security.
Below, you see the front cover of the booklet published by the
NFA, called "Opportunity and Risk: An Educational Guide
to Trading Futures and Options on Futures":

There is an illustration of a tightrope with one person
on it, and one safely across. The man on the tightrope looks
stable with an umbrella for balance, and he has an excellent
chance of making it across. The cover implies that, although

there is a risk of falling, investors can make it safely across.

This is deceptive and in no way accurately describes the risks of the commodity markets. The illusion is that, despite the risk, there is always a positive outcome. The pamphlet's authors use the title "Opportunity and Risk" as though those two elements are equal, but they fail to provide any statistics to give us any sense of what is more likely to happen.

If the illustration were accurate, here's how the cover should look:

Opportunity (5 percent) and Risk (95 percent)

In the bottom of the "pit," there should be a large collection of bodies of those who didn't make it. To be accurate, the illustration should show people continually the pit. And the person on the rope shouldn't look secure or stable at all. Now, while this may not be the marketing pitch the NFA wants to send out, it would better represent the risks involved in playing the commodities markets.

The NFA mission statement

When you open the booklet, you find the NFA mission statement on page two that says in part: "As a congressionally authorized self-regulatory organization, NFA's mission is to provide innovative regulatory programs and services that ensure futures industry integrity, protect market participants and help our Members meet their regulatory responsibilities."

Interesting. Let's look at that simple mission statement in more detail. It has been legally authorized by the government to regulate the commodity markets. With that in mind, if you remember my definition of a self-regulated organization, then you know that it creates rules and regulations with the goals of

- ensuring the success of the organization,
- ensuring the winners get their money,
- ensuring the losers can't hold the brokers and exchanges liable, and
- ensuring no records be published that are negative to the success of the organization.

Therefore from the very beginning you are told that the NFA is a self-regulated organization, and if the commodity markets no longer existed, the NFA and its employees would be out of a job. As long as everyone plays by the rules, the job of the NFA is to protect the markets from the investors and not the investors from the markets.

As I've said before, the fox is in charge of the hen house. The NFA promotes its "innovative regulatory programs" as exciting new ways to invest in commodities. The organization touts tightly controlled rules. All of this, its public relations people say, is designed in the investors' best interest. Of course, it's all an illusion.

In fact, these "innovative regulatory programs" consist of a whole host of highly complex games designed to ensure a steady flood of losers with regulations to protect the brokers and exchanges from liability from the losers in the markets. It's the financial losers, not the winners, who keep the markets operating.

You are conditioned to believe that when the regulatory commissions create rules to "protect the investors," they are protecting the investors from losing their money from bad advice from brokers or financial advisors. The investors are, in fact, protected from acts that break the rules. But the rules are written to protect the exchanges from the investors, not to protect the losers from the exchanges. Nothing is written about how investors who lose in the market can get their money back when everyone plays by the rules. The losers support the winners, and the losers in the market have no legal recourse. So how can that work in the best interests of the investors?

"Market integrity" is another interesting term here. It gives you the impression that the markets are a fair place to do business. But the rules are written to protect the exchanges, and the only thing the investor is protected against is anyone breaking the rules. This is far from "fair," since a vast majority of investors lose money in the markets. The NFA doesn't publish the fact that investors are participating in a minus-sum game, or that the markets depend on the losers on the market to survive.

The NFA does ensure that everyone plays by the rules, and brokers will talk about how tough these rules are. But they are primarily designed to collect margin money to guarantee that the winners get their money. This way, the markets can claim "market integrity," brokers can brag about following the rules, and the investor has a false sense of security that his or her best interests are being taken care of.

What the NFA booklet tells you . . .

The NFA booklet is full of general quotes that have no factual basis. For example, on page six of the booklet, you see the following: "For nearly a century and a half, markets have fulfilled an important economic function: providing an efficient and effective mechanism for the management of price risks."

This is simply not true, as it is neither efficient nor effective. When you look at the billions of dollars that are in motion every day in the market, with the prices constantly changing, how is that efficient? If a majority of people are buying and selling contracts, and a majority of contracts purchased are not delivered, how is this process beneficial for anyone but a select few?

Weak words

Both the NFA and the financial industry in general are infamous for vague rhetoric. A "built-in disclaimer" is created to avoid commitment to any statement.

If you read the NFA booklet, you will see the following weak words used continually:

- can,
- should or should not,
- possibility,
- possibly,
- potentially,
- in light of ,
- in part, and
- may or may be.

Here's a typical sentence on page eight of the booklet, describing the steadfast confidence that the NFA has in your playing the commodity markets:

"For those individuals who fully understand and can afford the risks which are involved, the allocation of some portion of their capital to futures trading can provide a means of achieving greater diversification and a potentially higher overall rate of return on their investments."

In fact, when you read the whole booklet, you can't find anything concrete. This isn't isolated to the NFA booklet. Just read or watch any financial services commercial and see if you can spot all of the weak words. With these weak words, marketers give the reader an illusion of commitment. From my perspective, here's the difference:

> You *will* win a million dollars.
> You *can* win a million dollars.

Which one locks me into a commitment? Using weak words prevents the speaker from being locked in to any statement, and you can't legally depend on or draw a conclusion from the statement. This allows the NFA to avoid actual accountability and responsibility. And it shifts the blame solely to the investor.

The NFA booklet also describes how investors provide "an active liquid and competitive market." What this means is that a liquid market ensures that there are sufficient contracts outstanding and adequate buyers and sellers to have enough money to cover large transactions without a substantial change in price.

The liquidity of the market comes from the margin money held in escrow and the number of people holding contracts. This margin money will guarantee that the winners get their money.

Today, with far less than 1 percent of all futures contracts dealing with actual commodities, it didn't take long for the markets to realize how they could receive additional money from investors. When market exchanges required both sellers and buyers to make a margin deposit, the commodities exchanges realized that much of this money would remain in their possession for days and weeks. Exchanges pay zero interest on margin money they collect from investors, creating an additional source of revenue at investors' expense. To put this into perspective, consider this: As of March 1, 2008, the New York Mercantile Exchange told me on the phone that they had $25 billion of margin money on hand. Now, at 5 percent interest, that is $1.25 billion generated before the doors even open. On the same day, the Chicago Board of Trade told me they had $2 billion on hand in margin money for just corn futures.

Just on the interest alone, the markets ensure their continuing success.

Price management

The NFA claims the commodities market uses price management to maintain a fair pricing of all commodities on the market. And this price management is beneficial to consumers by providing a strong economic function by keeping prices low. This is simply not true.

The markets become a plus to the producer and a negative to the consumer. Markets are restricted in the way they set prices by the parameters of what they call a "reasonable profit" and pricing it out of the market. This allows the producers to work from a baseline of reasonable profit and up. If the markets set prices too low, then the producers will remove the commodity from trading. The price has to stop going up when it prices the product out of the market. This is the parameter within which the markets work. Thus, when the consumer is charged a price above "reasonable profit," the consumer pays more because it means the producers have used the markets in their advantage to price their products above what they could normally charge.

In addition, a company that has products represented in the commodity markets can charge higher prices and use the commodity markets as a scapegoat. How? One of the first things you need to know is that a producer doesn't have to use the market price. The producer can sell it at any price it wants. But when the commodity markets drive the price up, the producers as a whole can use the markets to their advantage to gouge the consumer and avoid prosecution for price fixing, because they are using "market price." They manipulate the process in their best interest of higher profits instead of that of the consumer.

Let's use the popular topic of gas prices as an example. It is estimated that it costs approximately $40 per barrel of oil to bring it out of the ground and to market. At a reasonable 20 percent markup, that would be $48 per barrel, and gas prices would be around $2.00 per gallon. However, because crude oil prices are determined on the commodities market, the price this summer was driven up to an all-time high of $150 per barrel. Oil companies made record profits, yet they did so under the rules and without a credible threat of price-gouging because they were simply playing by the rules.

There was also a debate on the role of speculators in the record oil prices. Educated people on various news outlets spoke of supply and demand being the primary cause of the escalating oil prices, dismissing speculators as a market "boogeyman." However, it is interesting that when the speculators got out of the market in late summer of '08, oil prices dropped under $100 per barrel again. The speculators were not doing anything illegal, just operating under the loosening of regulations that happened in the 1980s. They were simply following the rules.

Guess what? The rules are wrong, and we're paying the price!

You've noticed that gas prices change daily or sometimes even a couple of times per day. There is no way this is a result of supply and demand, and it isn't a result of oil companies needing to raise prices to offset production costs to ensure they make a profit. Oil prices have to remain between "reasonable profit" and pricing the product out of the market. Our economy is very strongly petroleum-based, and so we are paying around $100 per barrel for oil (as of September, 2008) and almost $4 for a gallon of gas. OPEC doesn't meet daily to determine supply and demand. That shows that the oil companies set prices without fear of prosecution and make record profits.

I'm sure you don't know this, but producers are allowed to buy and sell commodity contracts of their own products, thus having an unfair influence on market price. This is an outrageous conflict of interest. How can an oil company be fair, equitable, and working for the consumer when they can manipulate the price in their best interest? This is another revenue stream for oil companies, especially if they know a shortage is coming and can manipulate the market accordingly. Congress needs to shut this barn door.

Look, I have no problem with companies making a profit. Just don't tell me that using the commodities market to determine prices is in the best interest of keeping consumer prices low. That is a falsehood. Why wouldn't a producer be involved in the commodity markets when they can get "reasonable profit" and above for their products? Any producer will not produce a product for long when they are losing money. They use the commodities market to create higher profits for themselves, blame the market process for the price increases, and the consumer pays higher prices.

The role of "reflecting" and "price discovery" on commodities prices

The commodity markets promote the fact that they manage price risk through reflecting and discovering prices, not by setting them. This is a very important difference, since it removes any responsibility for high prices from the producers and places it squarely on the market. But the producers claim that high prices are due to factors outside the control of the markets. This in and of itself is contradictory in nature. They claim this provides a very important economic function by keeping prices lower for the consumer. This is the key illusion and deception the exchanges use.

I called the Chicago Board of Trade and found out how many contracts were sold in one commodity (corn) in January 2008, and how many were delivered.

Number of corn contracts sold: 4,213,195.
Number of corn contracts delivered: 0.

The consensus of all of these contracts sold is how they determined the price of corn. This was how much motion and revenue was created in one month on one commodity. The fees and commissions on this motion are in the hundreds of millions of dollars. The margin money on hand for corn alone is almost $2 billion, which sits in escrow at the Chicago Board of Trade and earns interest, yet no one can tell you how that margin money is divided up.

I also contacted the New York Mercantile Exchange, and they gave me the following information about crude oil:

Number of crude oil contracts
sold in January, 2008: 10,814,818.
Number of crude oil contracts
delivered in January, 2008: zero.
Number of open-ended contracts: 1,392,370.

The consensus of all of these contracts sold is how they determined the price of crude oil, which consequently affects the gas prices you pay at the pump. This was how much motion and revenue was created in one month on one commodity. The fees and commissions on this motion are in the hundreds of millions of dollars. The NYME also revealed that they do not make public the amount of margin money on hand for crude oil, but as a whole exchange, they have about $25 billion on escrow collecting interest.

The NFA booklet says this about price discovery:

As the term indicates, futures markets "discover"—or "reflect"—cash market prices. They do not set them.

Now, logic would suggest that the term *reflect* would indicate that the price is already there to begin with. The term *discover* would mean the price is already there. However, according to the NFA:

Price Discovery – The determination of a price by a market process.

Reflect – The consensus of buyers and sellers opinions at that time.

So, by the NFA's own definition, prices are created through the consensus of the buyers and sellers. This is inconsistent with claims that prices are discovered.

Listen, the fact is the New York Mercantile Exchange does not call every gas station in the country every morning and ask them what their gas prices are to determine prices for oil contracts. Contracts are bought and sold based solely on individual contracts being sold with the intent to resell that contract at a profit. As a result, prices are set by the buyers and sellers of the contracts, not on the basis of supply and demand. OPEC does not meet daily to determine gas prices, and prices are not determined on current supply and demand.

The reason prices continually change is simple: For the exchanges to stay in business, the prices have to change constantly to create motion, which results in fees and commissions for the exchanges and brokers. The NFA even acknowledges that in the booklet:

"The process of reassessment (price discovery) is continuous" (p. 20), and ". . . The only certainty is that the price will change" (p. 21).

Myriad factors

By now, I hope, you understand how the commodity markets deceive the public by trying to convince us that prices are created primarily through supply and demand. In fact, prices that the mercantile exchanges establish are determined through the consensus of the buyers and sellers of the contracts. But if you read carefully, the NFA contradicts any possibility that supply and demand can be how prices are discovered. How? They use the term "myriad factors" to explain how prices increase and decrease through a wide variety of causes completely outside the control of the markets. This is important, since one definition of "myriad" is "an indefinitely great number."

When you hear on the news that commodities prices rose or fell on supply and demand or because of an act of nature, the actual fact is that there is an infinite number of factors investors use to determine market prices.

Let's review:

- Prices are "set" through the consensus of the buyers and sellers based on a myriad of factors.

- The markets do not "reflect" or "discover" cash market prices.
- Prices are created through individual investors' mental process using an infinite number of factors to outguess another investor in predicting an unpredictable to make money.
- Investors rely on their emotions and ego to establish a price instead of any scientific or mathematical formula.

Onions and diamonds

Sounds like two contradictory items (although I guess both can make women cry). So, why am I bringing these up? Well, in 1958, Congress removed futures trading for onions. And what happened since? In the fifty years since, onions have continued being harvested and sold. There has been no report of an onion shortage, nor have there been any reports that onion prices have been subject to excessive price increases in comparison to other commodities. The same can be said for tenderloins as well as any number of products not on the futures market. The price of onions remain constant and reasonable, their availability remains strong, and this was done without the "help" of the commodity markets.

What about diamonds? In this case, as of January 2008, the price of gold approached $900 an ounce for the first time. But what about the price of diamonds? Since they're not listed on the exchange, you'd have to check with your local jeweler. I would imagine that diamond prices have remained fairly consistent over the years and remain an important investment to a certain segment of the population.

It is argued that there is no futures market for diamonds because of the variations that exist from diamond to diamond. The real commodity, they claim, is carbon. However, the fundamental value of the carbon in a diamond is quite trivial. It is only when the carbon in a diamond is configured in a very specific way that the diamond then has value.

The diamond and onion markets have managed price risks all by themselves without any help, and both industries still appear to be thriving. The fact that some commodities are left off proves the markets can't claim to provide an important economic function if all products are not represented.

Price risk

Management of price risk: Speculators seek the price risk that hedgers seek to avoid.

Commodities markets always talk about risks. This is another brilliant move by Wall Street.

By talking about risks:

- The reward in business is payment for taking risks.
- The exchanges shift risk from one party to another.
- This shifting motion increases costs to our society.
- The reason is the cost of insurance is passed along to the consumer.
- Risk is what business is all about.

- The exchanges are playing on our instincts to seek financial security.
- In our search for security, we are vulnerable to the exchanges' plan to avoid risk.

This transfer of risk generates another revenue stream by creating motion where none existed before. In the final analysis, you don't avoid risk; you just pay to shift it from party to another. And that cost is passed along to the consumer.

At the end of the day, the NFA booklet fails to reveal any statistics about the true risks of the commodity markets and takes advantage of weak words to give you a false sense of security. If you read all ninety-three pages, you will notice that it fails to mention the exact number of investors who lose money, or how much, or how the margin money is divided up. In fact, you will be hard-pressed to find any real statistics at all. The authors never give you any percentages of failure or success. They never give you any percentage of winners to losers or a percentage of people who win money on specific commodities.

If the NFA were serious about protecting investors, it would demand full disclosure from exchanges of the following:

- how many investors lost money and how much;
- the brokers' honest account of the money lost by all of their investors;
- the amount of money that investors spent on fees, commissions and taxes; and

- how this affected the investors' overall performance.

Then investors as a whole would realize that they are not investing. They are gambling, playing games of chance with the odds firmly stacked against them.

This is why brokers won't give you a performance report, and that's why the commissions don't require such documents. To do so would be to expose the corridor to their success. Brokers who ballyhoo the success of their clients are blowing wind into the sail of a sinking boat.

7

The Hidden Truth about Hedging, Derivatives and Degree Days

"The derivatives genie is now well out of the bottle, and these instruments will almost certainly multiply in variety and number until some event makes their toxicity clear. Central banks and governments have so far found no effective way to control, or even monitor, the risks posed by these contracts. In my view, derivatives are financial weapons of mass destruction, carrying dangers that, while now latent, are potentially lethal."
—Warren Buffett, Berkshire Hathaway
annual report for 2002

I tried to make sure this book didn't get so complex you would lose the message, but I need to mention hedg-

ing, derivatives, and degree days. These are some of Wall Street's most brilliant revenue generators. Like all illusions and deceptions, they seem complex. However, when exposed, they are simple ways to bring new investors into the game and new infusions of cash into Wall Street.

Hedging replaces speculating under the illusion of solving a problem that Wall Street itself created. The problem Wall Street created was volatility in the markets. This volatility was created by constantly changing prices. The market has now created an environment where the producers of a commodity believe they have to protect themselves from this volatility. What draws the producer (an investor who produces a commodity) into the system is his search for security. The producer also believes that speculating has a positive outcome in that it provides insurance against this insecurity by avoiding adverse price changes. It's called hedging, but in reality, it's gambling.

Producer: Someone who actually is in charge of bringing the commodity (corn, oil, grain, etc.) to market. Farmers are the most well-known producers, but it could be other providers as well.

Contract market: A market in which commodity contracts are bought and sold without the need for delivery of the product.

Cash market: A market to which you take your commodity to sell for cash.

If the producer of a commodity gets more money from the commodity contract than his cash crop would have brought, then he considers himself a winner. If he loses money, the exchanges convince him that he did not lose; he just covered (offset) his losses with his cash crop. At this point, he feels satisfied that he has insured his product against adverse price changes.

In fact, Wall Street has now pulled him into a minus-sum game in which he will lose money on most of his contracts. The producer is gambling by participating in a solution, called "hedging," to a problem that the markets themselves created. And since the producer is largely unaware of the web of illusion and deception he's been drawn into, the process keeps going on. Every contract he purchases creates motion, which takes money out of his pocket and puts money in the pockets of the exchanges.

When you buy a commodity contract, you are a gambler, making a bet, period. That's as simple as it gets. To keep from getting confused, you've got to understand that when you purchase a contract, it is a completely separate function from selling a product on a cash market. No matter how you look at it, when you buy and sell a contract, you will either make money or lose money. And when you sell your product on the cash market, you will either make money or lose money. The only connection between a corn contract and a corn producer is the use of the word "corn." You don't have to be a corn producer to buy a corn contract. Again, they are two separate entities mutually exclusive of each other. The brilliance of the plan is how they are tied together.

The exchanges have convinced producers that if they lose money in the commodities market, they didn't really lose it, they just offset it with their cash crop. What this means is that they've convinced the producers to gamble by purchasing on a contract, and if they lose money, then the money brought in will make up for the money lost on the contract. In actuality, their cash crop brought the price the market offered, and the contract was bought and sold separately. The producers believe they broke even, when in fact, they have lost money.

By falling into this illusion, producers are led to believe that cash contracts and commodities contracts are intertwined. They are deceived into believing that by offsetting, they can protect against losses on their cash crop. They are tricked into participating in gambling games and calling it insurance. The reality is that markets don't care where you get the money to pay them. The gambler who lost money on his bet knows he lost money. The producer who loses money on his corn contract believes that the price for his corn crop offsets his losses. In both cases, there is negative money for the investors. With two similar but separate entities intertwined, producers are seduced into participating. Wall Street has successfully deployed yet another brilliant marketing strategy.

What draws investors to the game?

The two main components of the commodities market are constantly changing prices and buying and selling by the second. A producer is lured in by his search for financial security and is tempted by the prospects of taking a little money and turning it into a lot of money quickly, without effort.

These prices are always changing because of buying and selling based on myriad factors including the judgment and emotions of the investors. This volatility keeps investors' money in motion. And the market itself creates the volatility that results in constantly changing prices. With everyone guessing about the changing prices, producers and investors alike are drawn in by using factors other than supply and demand.

As a reminder: This is how a producer/investor can possibly—but not probably—turn his or her money quickly in the stock market:

If you plug any number into the equation and do the math, you can see the appeal.

Margins are an added lure to bring players to the tables. They have no use other than to draw the players in to a pure gambling scenario. A margin is a portion paid of true value, which in the commodities markets comes out to approximately 1/20th. By putting up 1/20th of the value of a commodity, players can make 20 times return of its true value. This allows investors to turn a little money into a lot of money quickly without effort.

Now, I'll show you the same formula using margin money: Margins also make it possible to sell the contract and buy back more than you sold with the same money. For example, if corn is $2.00, and margins are 1/20th you pay 10 cents in margin $ to buy a bushel of corn ($2.00/20+10 cents). If corn goes up 10 cents, you can sell it for 20 cents, and take the 20 cents and buy two bushels of corn for the initial investment of 10 cents.

Again, as I mentioned earlier, this potential to continually double your money, despite the risks, is what draws investors into their web . In creating "hedging," the brilliance of Wall Street is that they

- changed "speculating" into "hedging";
- created a problem that didn't exist;
- created a solution to the problem they created;
- convinced producers that they weren't gambling, but instead they were insuring your product;
- allowed producers to use margin money in hopes of turning a little money into a lot of money quickly; and
- turned the negative performance of speculating into an illusion of a positive outcome of hedging for the producer.

You have to admit, this is pretty ingenious on the part of Wall Street. They're teaching you that you're insuring a positive with a negative. And the truth is producers will not produce a product for long, at a loss financially. The process is positive to the producer and negative to the consumer.

So, why do you need the markets?

Derivatives

Wall Street, like all businesses, is always on the lookout for additional revenue streams. As a result, Wall Street figured out that, like casino-goers, some people are willing to bet on anything. With this in mind, operators of the commodity markets took advantage and expanded their games to allow investors to risk their money on an array of intangibles and insignificant events.

Derivatives are considered a financial contract between two parties that are linked to the performance of assets, interest rates, currency exchange rates, or indexes. This allowed the commodities market to expand from corn and oil to nontangible items such as degree days and cell phone minutes. The exchanges call these derivatives. Derivatives are the most transparent example of gambling in its purest form.

By introducing derivatives, the number of items on which to buy and sell contracts has expanded tremendously, as well as the number of investors willing to risk their money on these new games. As a result, there was more than $516 trillion in derivatives contracts circulating in March, 2008, according to the most recent survey by the Bank of International Settlements, the world's clearinghouse for central banks in Basel, Switzerland. The fact is that this is all perceived value. There's no money there.

An entire book can be written on derivatives. The fact that experts in finance, including Warren Buffett, have trouble properly defining what derivatives are and how they work proves that Wall Street got it right. I define a derivative as anything that can be assigned a value that has a perceived effect on someone's profit or loss.

Facts about derivatives

- Derivatives are an extension or evolution of Wall Street to keep money in motion by creating an al-

most unlimited amount of new revenue streams.
- This creates a perceived value with no money to back it up.
- Under false pretenses, derivatives claim to have a positive economic value.
- It is a minus-sum game to investors.
- The more motion that is created, the less money investors have, and the more money Wall Street accumulates without producing anything of value.
- This creates an unstable economic environment. (this was originally written in March, 2008 before the Financial Crisis hit in September.)
- If the government can't understand derivatives, then they can't regulate them, so they need to do away with them.

The brilliance of Wall Street's plan is that by using intangibles, they have been able to sell the concept that derivatives are another way to hedge risk.

Honestly, derivatives are nothing more than gambling games, just another way to separate money from the masses and place it in motion. Almost anything can be used as a point of reference for purchasing a contract to try to outguess another investor. At the end of the day, derivatives contribute no more economic value to the country than playing Texas hold-em poker provides an economic value to Texas.

Derivatives are basically a casino on steroids where securities which have no intrinsic value but instead represent bets on other securities, which are traded for ridiculously high paper profit. When that house of cards falls, it will likely take much of the larger economy with it. Pension funds, banks, brokerages, and other institutions holding worthless hedge fund paper are forced under by tremendous losses.

Degree days

Degree days are another outrageous example of what investors can bet on in the commodities markets. We know playing the commodities market can involve everything from traditional examples like oil and corn to newer games like cell minutes and band-width. An absurd concept, offering the buying of futures contracts based on various weather-related events is highly popular in commodity markets.

Here's a partial list:

Clean Air Degree Days Index, Atlanta
Degree Days Index, Boston
Degree Days Index, Chicago
Degree Days Index, Cincinnati
Degree Days Index, Dallas
Degree Days Index, Des Moines
Degree Days Index, Kansas City
Degree Days Index, Las Vegas
Degree Days Index, Minneapolis
Degree Days Index, New York
Degree Days Index, Philadelphia
Degree Days Index, Portland
Degree Days Index, Tucson
Seasonal Degree Days Index, Atlanta

Seasonal Degree Days Index, Las Vegas
Pacific Rim Index, Osaka
Seasonal, Pacific Rim Index Tokyo
Heating Degree Days, Amsterdam
Seasonal Heating Degree Days, Berlin
Monthly Heating Degree Days, Berlin
Seasonal Heating Degree Days, London
Monthly Heating Degree Days, Paris
Monthly Heating Degree Days, Paris
Seasonal Heating Degree Days, Stockholm
Seasonal Temperature Cumulative Average, Stockholm

What in the world are investors betting on when they take a position on these various weather futures contracts?

Wall Street has created an almost unlimited way for investors to hand over their money and made it so complex as to keep them involved. Each level of complexity and each new game brings in new investors and creates motion. Believe me, if you look at the number of combinations of shares or contracts you can purchase, this is just the tip of the iceberg.

8
The Hidden Truth of Wall Street's Plan

We have all heard the success stories; here's a story from someone who got taken in by the hype:

"Well, my name is Dave. I began involvement in the stock market in 1999. At first I was buying all kinds of different stocks that were being touted in I-net websites. The vast majority of the time I ended up losing money, sometimes lots of money. Eventually, if you hit someone over the head often enough, you quit playing. Which is what I decided to do . . . but only for a while.

"My problem was that I kept thinking that it was something wrong I was doing in my investment decisions. Eventually, I stumbled upon a Yahoo message board of a company I maintained a small number of shares in. I was losing on that

stock too, but I happened to read more, much, much more about this particular company (ticker ALU, now bankrupt). I began to learn about PE ratios and other fundamentals that I was not aware of. One poster had the most to say about ALU, and I became more confident about buying larger amounts of shares as the stock declined. Eventually, I owned about 20,000 shares.

"After I did my largest purchases, I called the company and spoke to a PR firm hired by said company. It dawned upon me (finally) that it really didn't make sense why stocks went up or down on a daily basis—even after earnings reports or "news" of some sort, there was never any consistency about any particular stock going up or down

(I noticed that some went up after supposedly bad earnings, while others went down after good earnings). I told the PR rep lady that the entire thing seemed like a pyramid scheme. I said it tongue-in-cheek because I really did not want to believe that it was in fact such a scheme (especially considering my large position I know held in ALU). Her response?

"In a sort of sly but honest tone of voice she told me, 'That's riiiight. . . .'

"So I asked her, 'So how does a stock go up or down?'

"She replied, 'Well, do you have friends and family? Tell them to get in. . . .'

"At that point I was dumb struck. . .and very, very scared since most of my money was now tied up in nothing but a conniving pyramid scheme game! In the end, I got lucky, and actually got out with a profit that time.

"But foolishly, I continued to participate in the scheme. Eventually, I lost more money. However, around 2001 I read on various stock chat message boards about the concept of short selling. I then realized just how bogus the entire stock market was. Because when I studied the fundamentals of most companies, I realized that there were many totally worthless and other grossly overvalued companies trading at insane market caps. I then began short selling, and quit buying altogether. I had some success, some failures. But as time went by, I realized that the ones I covered at a loss had I been patient I would have ended up with profits as well. So, I then decided to go more heavily into shorting.

"After a while, I was up something like $35,000 at one point. I was then very confident. Though I didn't always win, I was successful most of the time. So then, I decided to short more heavily, the most obviously blatantly overvalued (and worthless) companies trading. Problem was, around that time, almost every other small time stock trader was learning the same things I already knew, and they too started shorting everything in sight. It was at that point that the shorting game blew up. The institutions who run the BID-ASK show then practically cornered all their shares between themselves, and (I believe) collusively decided to bid all their own junk back up. I ended up giving back my gains, and losing an additional $35,000 or so. I had had enough. I saw it was a controlled and rigged scam against the retail small-time traders versus the Institutions who have every weapon at their disposal. Indeed, while all the little small time do it yourself type stock traders were shorting, the Fed mysteriously continued to lower interest rates to almost nothing in the face of economic data that clearly showed that no such action was warranted.

"But not one to give up hope, I stumbled upon other financial chat boards that presented a number of companies paying fat dividends, a very enticing concept considering where interest rates were at the time. So, I began buying some of these stocks in a small way. I was buying mostly MREITS, bond funds, municipal bond funds, and oil transporting companies. In the beginning I was getting big dividends and often time the stock prices were going higher. I was making my money back at last. As I gained more confidence, once again I went overboard and bought more heavily, especially in one MREIT, ticker NFI. I was up about $30,000 again and felt good and confident; my retirement was going to be great because of all of those dividends. Or so I assumed.

"Eventually, the prices started to dip. But I felt so confident, that I just kept buying those dips. I wasn't about to be 'shaken out.' To make a long story short, I bought so many dips that I ended up losing about $150,000 in very short order. The Fed this time mysteriously began raising rates to levels way beyond I think anyone's expectations. The excuse that it was the Fed's fault for causing the real estate debacle was now in place. In the mean time, the insiders of these companies I lost so much of my money in were still taking their fat salaries and cashing out their stock options.

"I then remembered what the PR rep lady told me years ago, about the stock market really being a pyramid scheme. I should have not only listened, but acted by staying out of the scam altogether. It was my fault, but I accuse the entire system of fraudulently hyping itself as something more than an ongoing institutionally controlled BID-ASK pyramid scheme, where only the insiders, fund manager/brokers, and perhaps a wealthy few of the latter's clients who get the inside scoop end up making a real cash profit in the "long term." Sure, you can win. Just like I did. But when you win some, you get confident. You think everything is on the up and up. So of course you don't quit while you are ahead. Of course you play more and more, until you end up losing not only your gains, but your principles as well. I may have been a fool, but the system is, as you say, an incredibly ingenious con created by people with tremendous skills and wisdom and conning you into their game. So am I the only one to blame for my losses? No, the con men who set up the system should not be permitted to continue their systematic psychological financial control game that they call 'The stock/ bond/commodities markets.' It's all just a preplanned extremely clever manipulation scheme invented by the wealthy few to try to lure in the majority of non-wealthy into their game with their ultimate goal of taking outsider's monies. And then after their game is eventually over, which could take decades, they will have their excuses ready so as to pin the blame on something other than themselves to try to pacify the angry masses who end up losing."

The distressing thing is that all across the country there are countless people like Dave who were conned out of their money, although most are too embarrassed to do anything about it. The fact that Wall Street insiders know and exploit this is a travesty.

By now, you have realized that you are a mark, participating in a con designed to separate you from your money. But who is responsible for setting this system up and keeping it going?

To understand how you have been conditioned and manipulated over the years, you have to understand how this was put into place.

There are five basic ways to acquire money:

1. Profting from production or sale of a product
2. Providing a service
3. Receiving a gift
4. Stealing
5. Manipulating

Wall Streeters have set up an entire system based on manipulating money from the masses without producing any goods or services. As I said in the introduction, entire books can and have been written about various individuals who helped put this system into place. If the system works to your advantage, you're going to work hard to keep it in place. You would train your successor to keep it going in their time. That's why it's not important to concern yourself with individual names; they're just people who made it to the top of their field and found out that they had to work hard to keep the money rolling in. In their quest, this group has spent generations studying and understanding human behavior. As a result, they perfected a system to con the masses out of their money without question, prosecution, or accountability. They are masters of illusion and deception.

Over time, they developed such a complex system that the masses do not understand it; the media and academic world promotes it; the government cannot control or regulate it properly. Therefore, Wall Street insiders continue to perpetuate their scam, and as it gets bigger and bigger they satisfy their addiction to wealth at the investors' expense.

I have to give them credit. I'm extremely impressed with their abilities. This process did not happen overnight. It began with the conception of markets and has evolved and developed over the course of generations. Wall Streeters have developed an incredibly sophisticated and confusing system to keep the scam going. How is it that they scam us out of billions of dollars a day without question? They've convinced us to believe that, by following their system, you can turn a little money into a lot of money without effort.

How did they implement their system to pursue greed without remorse?

1. They had to change your mindset from the idea of playing gambling games to performing a very vital economic function by investing your money.

2. They created a system that was complex; the news media supports it; the academic world teaches it; elected officials have legalized it; and the masses believe in it unquestionably and without demand for accountability.

3. They convinced regulatory agencies to make rules so complicated that only a select few can understand them.

4. They designed it so no one would ask for a performance report from brokers and exchanges, and the government would not require it.

5. They created a system in which no one knows, questions, or appears to care where their winnings come from.

6. They deceived us into believing the terms "published value," "perceived value," and "outperformed" represented real value. They are words of illusion and deception.

7. They created a problem that did not exist and offered "hedging" as a solution to the problem.

8. They created such a complex web that even if one part is damaged or removed, another quickly replaces it.

9. They promoted the market as being an essential part of the economy to the point that anyone who challenges the system is "anti-American" or "anti-capitalism."
10. They created the ultimate scam by convincing us that it is our fault we lose money by playing their con games.

The brilliance of the ultimate con is that, like a majority of us, you take responsibility for your losses. You do not seek retribution from the brokers or demand that our elected officials step in on your behalf. And even if you tried, the system is set up to protect Wall Street, not the investor.

The use of psychology and behavioral finance on Wall Street

If I were to run a gambling organization, the most important thing I would do is take a course in human behavior. The casinos, markets, and exchanges knew this early on and have become experts in understanding the psychology behind to separating investors from their money without question.

Wall Streeters have spent untold amounts of money researching human behavior and perfected ways to take advantage of every human weakness to separate the masses from their money. They have spent years studying and applying the science of human nature to convince you to trust them by convincing you it is "investing." Why do they spend so much time studying psychology?

The answer is simple: Wall Street markets alone controls approximately $8.4 trillion of your money. For every 1 percent they can skim off the top through fees and commissions, they stick another $84 billion in their pockets. Derivatives in the commodity markets account for $300 trillion. One percent off the top is $3 trillion. Approximately $2 billion in commodity contracts are traded per day. Do the math; count your money.

Their researchers uncovered that playing the markets, like gambling, is based on irrational behavior. We make decisions based on emotion rather than logic or information. This makes your minds easy to manipulate because Wall Street insiders tap into our desire for financial wealth and security. And this conditioning through illusion and deception has gone on for decades. Now, they started using new psychological technologies of what they called "behavioral finance." Wall Street discovered that people are excited to be in on the latest system, and they've developed programs to use your enthusiasm against you. Again, all of the money spent is a drop in the bucket compared to what they can earn by keeping your money in motion. Trust me, they are not working with your best interests in mind.

Like any good ad campaign developed on Madison Avenue, every investment ad you see or sales pitch you hear is a result of proven psychological and marketing tricks developed by Wall Street. In order to get their hands on your money, they use proven visuals and spokesmen to convince you that you are not gambling and are not taking an unacceptable risk.

Remember, it makes no difference to them if you win money or lose money, only that you keep your money in motion.

Wall Streeters play with investors' minds on two levels: novice investors are convinced that investing is "safe." Your insecurities are intensified when you are convinced that, if you're smart and listen to the right people, you can accumulate wealth quickly. (And oh, by the way, it will be mentioned in passing that you can lose all of your money. However, if you listen to their advice, that won't happen to you.)

So, let's be clear, Wall Streeters use tricks of Vegas, Madison Avenue, and psychologists to engage in a psychological war on the minds of average Americans trying to hold on to their retirement savings.

They use the three C's, Camouflage, Conditioning, and Convincing, to separate investors from their money:

- They *created* an illusion and deception to camouflage risk so investors will believe their money is safe.
- They *condition* investors to believe that stocks and commodities are vital to the economy.
- They *convince* investors that they are only looking after their best interests.

They do this by changing your mindset from gambling to investing, speculating, hedging, and trading. But one thing is for certain—you are their prey.

The objective of Wall Street insiders is to create a dependent investor, not an informed investor. Remember, they do not care if you win money or lose money, only that you continue to keep your money invested. They only care about keeping investors' money in motion. They know investors as a whole are poorly educated about how to play the markets. They also know most investors are insecure, vulnerable, and often irrational. They know investors are easy to deceive, manipulate, and control. The investor wants to "win big," and Wall Streeters consistently exploit that desire to separate these innocents from their money.

Wall Street insiders keep the academic world working with them and supporting them by generously awarding consulting contracts, grants and retainers to hire the best talent in investment psychology (yes, there is such a thing) to work on perfecting the con to manipulate you. That guarantees Wall Street will achieve their target not only of developing dependent investors, but of recruiting the new blood needed to keep the markets going.

Don't believe me? Take a moment and look up the Nobel Prize winner for Economics in 2002. You may be surprised to discover that it was awarded to Daniel Kahneman, a psychologist, not an economist. It's as important to discover WHY you invest and WHAT makes you invest, as HOW you invest.

In the end, Wall Streeters set up a system that benefited those who upheld the status quo.

The advantages of owning a seat on the exchange

When you are an investor in the stock market, you rely on the information you have either researched yourself or have received from a broker or money manager. Both ways will provide you with outdated information the moment it hits your hand. Receiving current information is not possible as you are not legally allowed access to inside information. When stock information finally trickles down to you, the info has been old news for about six months.

Yet, there are those who will purchase a seat on the New York Stock Exchange for as high as $4 million. Common logic would suggest that spending millions of dollars to get access to a seat on any exchange provides enormous advantages that are worth the money spent.

Owning a seat on the NYSE enables one to trade on the floor of the exchange, as an agent either for someone else (floor broker) or for one's own personal account (floor trader).

What do these people get in return for this seat?

1. They have immediate access to information an average investor does not have, resulting in instantly profitable decisions for the seat owner.
2. They do not have to pay fees, resulting in larger profit margins than average investors.
3. They can collect fees from other investors.
4. They can move swiftly on slight changes in price.

5. They can secure bailouts from the government (and taxpayers) when they make continually poor business decisions.

The price paid for a seat on the NYSE gives the owner substantial advantages. They have instant access to information, which benefits them immediately. This instant access to information may only gain brokers an advantage as small as pennies per stock, but by buying huge amounts without having to pay fees, they benefit by millions of dollars.

Average investors are at a substantial disadvantage. They are making calculations with nothing more than outdated information. Investors have to pay fees and commissions on each movement. The playing field just gets more and more slanted.

It's important to remember two things:

1. These examples are only part of the multitude of advantages Wall Street insiders use to work the system in their favor.
2. As we associate playing the markets with the gambling, we see these advantages ensure that the average investor is always running as hard as he can with no hope of catching up.

It's bad enough that investors are automatically engaged in a minus-sum game, but the system allows for the powerful and influential to have added advantages. If Congress demanded full disclosure and accountability, then more pressure would be placed on the exchanges and corporate boards to end these unfair practices.

The hidden truth about the media as part of Wall Street

Whatever your views on the media, whether you think there is a "left-wing bias" or a "vast right-wing conspiracy," you need to believe one thing: The media is fully in the pocket of Wall Street insiders and power brokers. I don't think it's evil, just simple economics and ignorance. The media's livelihood depends on ratings, readership, ad revenue, and good will from a strong financial market. Positive coverage gets more access to the power brokers. Plus, they continue getting invited to all the best parties. As I've said, the system is so complex, that the "talking heads" who cover the markets are reading the same cue cards as your local newscaster.

The national media's promotion of a healthy market is in their own best self-interest. You are relentlessly battered with information about the markets: stock market updates on the radio and television, business section of the local paper, cable channels devoted solely to daily coverage of every bit of news related primarily to New York Stock Exchange, NASDAQ, the Chicago Board of Trade, and the New York Mercantile Exchange. It's enough to boggle the most discerning mind.

If you read any ad, profile or story about the stock market or financial planning, you'll notice there is a rhythm to the story. The cadence leads readers along a path covering the risks and past the disclaimers to get to a place they want them to go. At the end, you're led to their web by their use of weak words, disclaimers and statements instead of statistics. They can claim "honesty" in their "hard-hitting" story while you dismiss the risk and focus on your eagle's eye view on what you've been conditioned to believe.

The funny thing is I believe the majority of the media types who cover the markets have no idea of their true nature. This blissful ignorance by media members of the markets ensure they keep their job while being an accomplice (willing or unwilling) of Wall Street insiders' marketing program.

The end result is a persistent daily blitz of news, 99 percent of which is conditioning through exaggeration and promotion, and 1 percent reality. The news is spun by Wall Street's PR machine to influence investors to continue to hand over their hard-earned money and keep it in motion.

The media just puts out the propaganda that they are furnished. At no time does the media publish how much money investors have to lose every day to keep them all in business.

In the eyes of the media there are no red states or blue states when covering the markets, only green.

The absurdity and brain trickery of the Dow Jones and S&P 500

Every day, you read and hear about how the Dow Jones Industrial Average (DJIA) and Standard & Poor's (S&P 500 is used in reference not only to the index but also to the 500 actual companies, the stocks of which are included in the index) performed for the day with the information sometimes leading the news. It is hyped, promoted, obsessed over, and followed passionately, but let me ask you a question: What, exactly, IS the Dow Jones Industrial Average?

The hidden truth about the Dow Jones index

If I asked people on the street about the Dow Jones, few, if any, could give me an accurate answer. The Dow Jones is a reporting device that tracks thirty companies on the NYSE and uses this to estimate overall "trends" in the market for over 11,000 total companies on the exchange. That is a statistical average of 0.0027 percent of all of the listed companies.

Yet, you hear about it daily, and cable channels, newspapers, and magazines are dedicated to following its every move. But what is not reported is how you are deceived into believing that the Dow Jones has any value to investors. The simple fact is that it has no value.

The truth is that the Dow Jones is simply a tool Wall Street insiders promote as a motivating device to give investors a statistical point of reference every day to work from. The fact that the daily numbers are meaningless is not reported by the media. The Dow Jones can add or remove companies at their discretion and to the benefit of their report.

Market experts will admit that the daily numbers are not important but suggest focusing instead on "trends." Although you've been taught to believe, without question, that the Dow Jones is vitally important, there is no formula that shows how the Dow Jones can make you money. There are also no statistics available that show you that the Dow Jones has any value to investors.

Every day we hear and read whether the markets are up or down. We hear about what or where "investors" are looking for that particular day. There is no definition ever given as to who these "investors" are, or what percentage they represent of the 95 million investors. There is no explanation as to why opinions of the unnamed few are affecting the trends of the markets. Yet this doesn't prevent average Americans from getting concerned and making decisions based on the movement of the markets even though the companies reporting to Dow Jones have very little impact on their daily lives. The Dow Jones is the measurement of 0.0027 percent of listed companies and has no mathematical or scientific value in predicting the non-predictable or making money for investors as a whole.

If the Dow Jones went up 500 points, the media would celebrate, but if your investments went down at the same time (which is a real possibility) will you celebrate?

The Dow Jones is just another tool in the complex plan developed by Wall Streeters to create the illusion that it appears to have real value. Brokers use it to their advantage to show investors a chart depicting the rise of the markets over the years. A false sense of security is created among new investors, and that same fear keeps the investors who have already lost money.

If you look at any chart tracking the Dow Jones in the last thirty years, your first impression would be that the stock market has grown dramatically since 1980. Proponents of the markets will point to this chart as a positive. But the chart, like everything else the Wall Street insiders promote, is incomplete. What the chart doesn't show you is the number of companies removed from the exchange or the number of investors that made money or lost money during this time period. Wall Streeters have convinced us that the stock market has grown 10 percent a year on average, when in fact, that is a manipulation of statistics.

Here's a simple example of how Wall Streeters misuse statistics to convince us the stock market has grown 10 percent a year:

Let's say that in 1998, there are 100 listed companies.

From 1998–2008—they listed 220 new companies.

That should leave 320 listed companies, right?

What they don't tell you is from 1998–2008, 120 companies were removed from trading.

This leaves 200 companies; (100 +220)=320–120=200.

The markets report a 10 percent growth, but they don't explain the 120 companies that were removed from trading. Don't you wonder what happened to investors who had shares of stock in the 120 companies that were de-listed?

The hidden truth about the S&P 500

The S&P 500 is a measuring device used to track the trends of the top 500 publicly traded companies in the U.S. You would think that these are the cream of the crop. By investing in these high-end companies, you would believe that it has more added value than regular companies. The fact is that when you buy stocks in an S&P 500 company, like any other company, you have entered a minus-sum game. Your winnings come from losing investors, and your odds of winning are not improved over any other stock.

The risks involved in purchasing shares in an S&P 500 company are the same as any other stocks. You can't depend on the S&P 500 because the 500 are not consistent, and the values constantly change. The money an investor makes is not based on the performance of the company, but if you've outguessed other investors. At the end of the day, the investors who purchased S&P 500 stocks have less money in their pocket than when they started.

If the media were truly interested in reporting on the markets, they would not focus on meaningless indicators such as the Dow Jones and S&P 500. Instead, they would report on the amount of money individual investors lose on any given day.

The Dow Jones and S&P 500 are simply two of the myriad of factors used in determining prices. The average American doesn't know that the factors that determine the Dow Jones are constantly changing, and the companies listed in the S&P 500 are constantly changing. As a result, they have no real value; they are simply a statistical point of reference for reporting purposes.

In the end, those clawing their way up Wall Street's ladder are obsessed; addicted to wealth and power without remorse. As a result, they created a system that uses illusion and deception to bring in new investors and persuade old investors to keep their money in the markets with promises of long-term gains. They've spent the money and used the best psychological methods to camouflage the fact that you are gambling.

To perpetuate their power through the generations, Wall Street's power brokers have used their influence with politicians, lobbyists, Security and Exchange Commission staffers, corporate CEO's, money managers, reporters, bankers and even their own employees. They have convinced them that the system is beneficial to all, and they have conditioned you to believe, without question, that investors are not gambling and are not participating in a minus-sum game.

But the vast majority of investors are passive prey targeted by aggressive parasites that pretend to be acting in the nation's best interests. Wall Street's scam artists hide behind many masks, as brokers, planners, investment advisors, financial consultants, or money managers who are controlled by a system created solely to create revenue for a select few. It's a trap, and investors are their victims.

9
The Hidden Truth about Brokers

There's a reason I don't mention any specific names of Wall Street's power brokers. It's because you as an investor will more than likely never come into contact with them. You'll likely never meet them, hear about them, or hear from them. They live and work in a world different than most of us will ever see. However, the brokers, the people who look you in the eye and tell you to trust them with your money, live and work in your town. They may have limited contact with Wall Street as well, but they make a living based on the scam set up by their bosses.

You may think that brokers are professional money mangers who are working in your best interest. The truth is that they are trained as salesmen, not money managers, and their job is simply to make money for themselves, their bosses and the exchanges. The key is that brokers make more money off of investors that lose money than investors that make money.

Since the system survives on the losers in the markets, the job of brokers is to consistently work to keep the investors they have while recruiting new blood. Brokers get new investors by focusing their potential clients on money-making clients (if they have any), and keep meeting their quota by concentrating on keeping their losing clients involved. How can they do that if a majority of investors lose money? To do that, they need to mislead us.

When brokers are trained, they are taught proven and manipulative psychological tricks along with financial information. They may promote themselves as "investment advisors," but they are salesmen, first and foremost. As you might expect, a broker's so-called advice is self-serving and misleading. Anything they say and do enhances their efforts to close a sale. From their bosses they feel incessant pressure to perform. It's rolling down all the way from the top. Their primary directive from their boss is to get clients money in motion in order to generate commissions and fees.

In fact, the term *broker* has become such a dirty word that Wall Street insiders have begun to use different names for their sales force. *Broker* transformed into *investment advisor* or *financial consultant*, and they are there to provide "advice" to help investors manage their money not to sell you stocks or commodities contracts. And don't buy into the newest scam that brokers offer of no-fee services. What this means is that the fund managers are paying the commissions for bringing them clients, and believe me, the brokers know which ones are paying the highest commissions, and it has nothing to do with performance.

They convince you that they are working in your best interests when all they are doing is getting you to trust them to put your money in motion, and then making money off that motion. What this also does is allow brokers to utilize disclaimers and weak words to defend their position when you lose money.

Brokers and money managers don't tell you what to do with your money; they just give you "advice." They don't cause you to lose your money, they just "consult" with you. If you lose money, it was because you didn't take the advice of the broker, or the markets acted in a way beyond what the broker expected. Ultimately, they blame your losses on your ignorance and ultimately on you.

Look at the Financial Crisis of 2008, who does the media blame? They blame average people who were suckered into subprime (junk) loans and it's their fault that their dream of owning a house was exploited by greedy lenders and financial services firms. It's the classic Wall Street trick of blaming the consumer to divert attention away from their own manipulation of the rules.

How brokers mislead investors:

- They use the eagle's eye view.
- They use weak words.
- They use words that have no value.
- They use misleading information.
- They use propaganda of company performance.
- They use the lack of, and/or manipulation of, statistics.

- They encourage "long-term" investing.
- They use lack of full disclosure and accountability to mislead investors.

The manipulation of statistics

Here's an example of how an enterprising broker can manipulate statistics to convince you as an investor that he has a way to beat the system as he tries to convince you to trust him with your money. Working from a theory he is perfecting, the broker calls 1000 investors about his newest way to beat the system. He calls it "The Coin-Flip Method." The broker promises big returns to 500 of them if they take his expert advice and choose Mutual Fund A (aka "heads"). The other 500 he also promises big returns by following his expert advice and choosing Mutual Fund B (aka "tails"). "Tails" wins.

So the broker calls those 500 winners, promising 250 of them big returns if they follow his advice and chooses "heads," as a winner (and he was right on "tails") and the other 250 big returns by following his expert advice by choosing "tails" as a winner (and he was right on "tails"). The coin is flipped, and it's "heads," so the broker calls 250 investors . . . and so on. For one lucky investor, the broker is right ten times in a row!

His success inspires the broker to publish a book called "The Coin-Flip Method." In it he claims his system "produced 999 out of 1000 winners." But he hasn't given you all of the facts nor is he required to do so.

The broker can add the number of winners (500 + 250+125 and so on) and come out with a final number of 999. The broker can then claim that, out of 1000 investors there were 999 winners making his system as close to a "sure thing" as you can get. Right?

But, the actual numbers also tell you that 999 investors lost money, and that one investor out of a thousand was lucky enough to be the recipient of 10 lucky guesses. He also didn't tell you the fees and commissions and taxes involved in processing those bets. So, the true winner was the broker, especially with the book deal!

By focusing on the eagle's eye view, he can make a negative situation (999 out of 1000 lose) into a great situation (999 winners out of 1000 investors, or picking 10 straight winners). And to that one lone investor, the broker is a genius who helped make him wealthy.

According to the rules governing the markets, if this strategy is applied knowingly and with intent to defraud, it is illegal. However, the burden of proof is on the investor who never has all the necessary information. What happens in the "Coin-Flip Method" is the same thing that happens millions of times a day in the markets as brokers claim they can predict an unpredictable in your favor. Brokers are not trained to understand the markets and pick the best stocks, because there is no system. They are salesmen helping insecure investors try to turn a little money into a lot of money without effort. They're predicting an unpredictable, and if you still don't believe me, just remember these words:

"Past performance does not predict future results."

The scam analogy, made popular in the 1988 book *Innumeracy*, written by John Allen Paulos, appears in numerous books with similar versions and appears relevant in many ways to investors. Some books begin with sharing the information that many mutual fund companies offer numerous mutual funds. Did you ever consider that the more funds, or products, a company offers the better the chances are that one of the funds will rank at the top of its category? The company can then focus its marketing efforts on those funds that have "outperformed" others while keeping quiet about the funds that underperformed. In succeeding periods, different funds will rise to outperform others with marketing efforts shifting to those funds, like a game of hop-scotch.

How brokers use the eagle's eye view to manipulate statistics

Let me give you an example of how brokers mislead you to give you a false sense of security in playing the markets.

Example 1: Investor A purchased a share of stock from a company for $100

Out of pocket money	*In pocket money*
Investor A $100	sells to Investor B for $110
Investor B $110	sells to Investor C for $120
Investor C $120	sells to Investor D for $130
Investor D $130	
Total out of pocket	−$460
Total in-pocket	$360
Total out of pocket	−$100

In this example, Investor A, B and C all made money (after fees and commissions), and Investor D is -$130. Investors as a whole are -$100 + expenses.

Example 2: Investor A purchased a share of stock from a company for $100

> *Out of pocket money*.....................................*In pocket money*
>
> Investor A $100..........................sells to Investor B for $90,
>
> Investor B $90...........................sells to Investor C for $80,
>
> Investor C $80...........................sells to Investor D for $70,
>
> Investor D $70
>
> Total out of pocket.. −$340,
>
> Total in-pocket $240
>
> Total out of pocket.. −$100

In this example, all investors have lost money. Investor D is −$70. Investors as a whole are −$100 + expenses.

Example 3: Investor A purchased a share of stock from a company for $100

> *Out of pocket money*.....................................*In pocket money*
>
> Investor A $100..........................sells to Investor B for $100
>
> Investor B $100 ....sells to Investor C for $100
>
> Investor C $100..........................sells to Investor D for $100
>
> Investor D $100
>
> Total out of pocket...$400
>
> Total in-pocket $300
>
> Total out of pocket.. −$100

In this example, all four investors lost money once you take out fees and commissions. The broker would avoid showing you this, but if he did, he would claim this is a zero-sum gain, but in fact, it is a minus-sum game. And the company got the money, and Investor D is $100. Investors as a whole are –$100 + expenses.

Example 4: Investor A purchased a share of stock from a company for $100

> *Out of pocket money*...*In pocket money*
> Investor A $100..........................sells to Investor B for $90
> Investor B $90............................sells to Investor C for $100
> Investor C $100......................... sells to Investor D for $90
> Investor D $90
> Total out of pocket...$380
> Total in-pocket $280
> Total out of pocket...–$100

In this example, Investor B makes $10, but Investor A, C and D are minus $110 (plus added fees and commissions). When the broker explains this, he would show that Investor B made $10, and Investor D has a $90 value. Investors as a whole are –$100 + expenses.

To clarify, the money the publicly traded company receives from the sale of a share is never reclaimed. Fees and commissions are factored into every transaction (motion). In every example above, there is no denying that it is a minus-sum game.

Notice the simple math of the system. You can add layer upon layer of complexity and terminology, but it always comes back to simple math. That's the minus-sum game, and it's impossible for investors as a whole to beat the system.

The broker will confidently point to the three investors in Example 1 and point out how they made money. The fourth investor has possession of a stock that has seen steady growth. The reality is that Investor D has spent $130 and has a piece of paper that has published value. He has in his hand the greatest illusion of actual wealth. By focusing on the eagle's eye view of individual performance, an illusion is created that Investors A, B and C made $30, and Investor D has $130 value. It looks like a positive outcome, but the investors are out $100, plus fees and commissions, and Investor D is holding an empty bag.

Investor D represents the millions of investors in this country that hold approximately $15 trillion of published-value stocks today. They have paper with published value and no actual money in pocket. What will happen to all of the Investor D's of the world? They pawn off their stock to Investor E, and the game goes on with created motion. But there'll always be someone who will end up holding paper with published value and no real money.

Investors spend time studying financial reports that may or may not be accurate. They are almost certainly outdated. All of the news reports and stock market analysis on certain companies can be studied, but when their analysis is wrong (as it is more often than not), they can claim that past performance does not predict future results.

So, when brokers work in your best interest and tell you to invest in an S&P 500 company they judge "safe," you have no more chance of your money being secure than any other stock. As we saw earlier, S&P 500 is just a statistical point of reference that the industry uses and offers no true value.

If you bring up the losses you or another investor incurs, brokers and even other investors will blame the investor's inept actions, citing Caveat Emptor (let the buyer beware). Or the investors are being greedy and stupid. Why blame brokers who only offered their advice? Investors aren't fully educated on the ups and downs of the markets so of course the investors will lose money when they act on their own or when the market forces are in flux. The broker is merely a salesman who only provides advice how to best spend money. You should be responsible enough to do your own research, because you decide to buy what they're selling. This is hogwash.

Brokers always tell you there's a risk, but also leave out key information. They use psychological tricks to play upon your ego or your search for security. They use well-tested sales techniques and manipulation to get you to put your money in motion. And while others may have lost money, it was surely due to the investor being poorly educated and relying on bad information. But hey, if you play the game right, you will make a fortune. Then they use a combination of disclaimers, disclaimers, and more disclaimers to remove liability if they get caught sharing bad information.

And this information results in you playing the minus-sum game.

Wall Street insiders have succeeded in creating such a complex system that not only do a select few truly understand, but you need a license to actually conduct business with the exchanges. The key is when brokers' advice becomes bad advice, they place the blame solely on the investor for acting on that same advice. They also avoid liability under the rules set up by the Security and Exchange Commission (SEC) and the National Futures Association (NFA).

Despite all that you hear about how brokers have to be licensed and face a mountain of laws and regulations in order to protect the investor, the rules are actually designed to protect the organizations from the investors. So amateurs are held responsible even when their losses can be attributed to advice they received from professionals.

Don't count on the regulatory commissions to protect you as an investor. The commissions need the exchanges to be in business to have a job.

Let's say laws were enacted that allowed brokers to be charged with malpractice. Your broker or money manager would tell you in detail about every risk involved in handing them your money from the volatility of the markets to how it's impossible for anyone to beat the system long term. Every disclaimer would be spelled out for you in person, and you would be told the percentage of success or failure. If brokers had these standards, investors would have a far better understanding of what was happening with their money. It would also greatly reduce the number of investors crippling Wall Street, which is why it will never happen.

Record of investors' money

Change will only be brought about when investors demand full disclosure and accountability. Brokers and exchanges promote the fact that they are tightly regulated, but they are not required to keep or disclose simple information that would inform investors that they are entering a minus-sum game.

True story:

I asked my accountant to get a record of investors' money from a broker for a major financial institution. The broker responded to his request by asking my accountant who I was, why I wanted this information, that I didn't need that information, and that he wouldn't give it to me anyway. The broker then told my accountant he should fire me as a client for asking such questions. Why would he be so unwilling to provide the information to the point of suggesting my accountant fire me?

It isn't complicated. I wanted accountability, pure and simple.

What I got was a classic example of how the brokers and exchanges are not required to provide any information that would be detrimental to their success. A record of investors' money would show investors where their money goes and where it comes from. It would demand full disclosure and accountability from those people that handle investors' finances.

If records of an investor's money existed, it would detail:

- how the money was distributed;
- how much money the company received;
- how much in fees and commissions were charged off the top by the brokers and exchanges;
- how much the IRS collected;
- how many investors made money; and
- how much and how many investors lost money.

A record of investors' money would expose the illusion that investors, as a whole, are benefiting from the stock market. The fact is that the majority of investors are losing money. But Wall Street insiders have conditioned us to trust the process, and we don't ask for information we wouldn't get anyway. What would a level playing field look like?

It's impossible in a minus-sum game to have more investors making money than losing money as a whole. So, no matter how good a system is, they have to produce more losing investors to support the winning investors as a whole. If any financial planner was required to provide you with a performance report, it would have to show that more investors lost money than made money.

Remember that when you are dealing with brokers, they are part of Wall Street's marketing plan, whether they are consciously aware of it or not. Whether your broker has your best interests in mind, the system itself is an elaborate con. Investors are participating in a minus-sum game. And brokers do not have to provide an accounting of who wins money and who loses money.

The next time you go and visit your broker, ask him to fill out this form for you:

Yearly Personal Report

Name: _____

Acct #: _____

Out-of-pocket expenses: $ _____

In-pocket expenses: $ _____

A. Out-of-Pocket expenses:	**B. In-pocket expenses:**
Purchases $ _____	Sales $ _____
Fees: $ _____	Settlements $ _____
Commissions: $ _____	Dividends $ _____
Total A: $ _____	Total B: $ _____
Total money out of pocket (N): $ _____ (Negative cash flow)	**Total money in pocket (P): $ _____** (Positive cash flow)
If A is bigger than B Subtract B from A	*If B is bigger than A Subtract A from B*

This information is an accurate accounting of the client's yearly transactions.

Broker Name: _____

Signature: _____

(Note: This does not factor in taxes) Each year, the exchanges would be required to provide this information to each client.

10

The Hidden Truth Revealed

"The stock market has no use for human wisdom and judgment."
—Michael Lewis, "Evolution of an
Investor," *Portfolio*, December, 2007.

I wasn't interested in including a lot of references in the book because I felt that they either didn't get it or they didn't tell me anything new. One day while we were working on the book, I stopped in the bank to sign some papers and picked up the December 2007 issue of *Portfolio* magazine. I read the profile on Blaine Lourd written by Michael Lewis and realized that this man reveals the hidden truth about how the markets actually operate.

I encourage you to go to the website (portfolio.com) and read the story. It tells you everything you need to know about

the market through the eyes of a gentleman named Blaine Lourd. Through his eyes you can see how Wall Streeters really operates. He says, "Wall Street, with its army of brokers, analysts, and advisers funneling trillions of dollars into mutual funds, hedge funds, and private equity funds, is an elaborate fraud." While he tells you it's a scam and con, he is also weaving a web to bring you into his new fund.

Lourd shows an inclination to be a con man when he admits that he wanted to be a success. How that happened, he didn't much care. He left Louisiana when his father's oil business, his anticipated inheritance, collapsed. He landed his first job at EF Hutton and prepared himself by learning how to peddle stocks to people he'd never met. The key was to bring up Warren Buffett's name early and often. Lourd himself points out that he never understood why his customers never fired him. Before long, he began taking the investors for granted. According to Lourd: "You had to get the second deal done before the first one went bad." And, according to Lourd, the first one always went bad. His boss told Lourd that his job was to turn his clients' net worth into his own. It was amazing to him how gullible the investors were.

His fortune changed when the business manager of the rock band, the Rolling Stones, gave him $13 million to invest. He decided to forgo his bosses' advice and put it into T-bills. Even though this was a secure investment for the band, this brought in little revenue for the firm. His bosses told him his decision didn't make any money for them, and they pressured him to make transactions rather than give what he considered safe investment advice asked for by his clients, the Rolling Stones. I would think that Lourd made the best decision for his clients, but as you can see, the only goal was to keep the money in motion to generate fees and commissions.

Lourd makes several admissions throughout the article. He reveals details about how much money managers make, but also uncovers how, as a group, they cannot outperform the market. He admits that he, like many of his successful counterparts, abused drugs and alcohol due in no small part to the guilt they have over taking advantage of their clients. "You can't continually hurt people and feel good about your-self," he mused. Lourd admitted that becoming a success in this industry was reason enough to hate himself.

In an amazing admission of society's permissiveness of the industry, no CEO at any bank that Lourd worked for, no money manager or director, no chairman of the board and no associates ever asked him how his clients were doing. They just congratulated him periodically on his high gross commissions. Through all of his work with major Wall Street firms, the nicest thing Lourd could say about himself is that he hadn't broken the law. He recalls the times he spent making people happy about his advice when they should have been furious. Lourd says: "I always thought there would be a place where the clients and the brokers wouldn't be compromised. But it was the same everywhere." He was a top 10 revenue producer for every firm that employed him, but his success was not based on making successful investment decisions. He said he worked harder than everyone else to bring new investors into the game.

More and more, Lourd argues that Wall Street is a part of an elaborate fraud. He was one of those who funneled trillions of dollars into hedge funds, mutual funds and private equity funds, all the time growing less and less confident in his ability to pick winning stocks or money managers.

The illusion that professional investment managers can beat the market is proven false time and time again throughout the article. Blaine read Charles Ellis' book, *The Losers Game*. Ellis said there is no such thing as a financial expert. Blaine figured out that the problem wasn't him or the firms where he worked. The problem was the entire system of Wall Street, in which people presented themselves as financial experts and were paid extravagant sums of money for their "knowledge."

Ellis argues that there is no such thing as financial expertise. As Lourd read the book, he realized his whole life is a lie. "Everyone around me is facilitating this lie." Lourd was in the top 30 out of 6000 Edward Jones employees. Then he went to work for A.G. Edwards and began telling his clients he shouldn't pick stocks for them or dump their money into actively managed mutual funds. Instead, he chose to put it all in index funds. For this service, he took an annual fee of one percent of their assets. A. G. Edwards was not happy with his decision. Even the United States government and the SEC wanted him to keep his accounts in constant motion. At that point, Lourd said, "I was done."

This is an important crossroad. In Hollywood, the story would turn out that the lead character would leave Wall Street and spend the rest of his career working to fix a corrupt system. But, this isn't Hollywood. The amazing thing is after all of the disillusionment of his association with the market, Lourd starts his own firm and contacts a firm to invest his funds.

The firm, Dimensional Fund Advisors (DFA), sold investors on the idea of passive investing. Founded in 1981, the firm was built on a simple idea: Nobody knows which stock is going to go up. Nobody knows what the market as a whole is going to do. However honest their motto is, the fact that they are still drawing investors into the markets indicates that they just figured out a better marketing plan.

According to the article, DFA bought and held baskets of stocks chosen for the sort of risk they represented. And they—along with the idea they embodied—were growing at a sensational rate. By the summer of 2007, the firm had an astonishing $153 billion under management, $90 billion of which had come from individual investors through a network of professional advisers.

Those preparing to join the thousands authorized to sell DFA's funds to investors imply their agreement. They're all salesmen, but salesmen peddling an odd idea: Don't listen to salesmen. DFA's entire firm premise is all about "Wall Street floats on bullshit." DFA employees never believe they possess special wisdom and judgment. As an investor, this should tell you something.

Early on, at DFA, they did not sell individual stocks, try to time the market, or suggest to an investor that it is possible to systematically beat the market. They sold investors on the premise that investors can't beat the system, and DFA can't beat the system, but they wanted your money anyway. And as one DFA person said: "Who would be the most efficient at taking investors who thinks he can beat the system in the markets and turn him into someone who quits trading and hands their money over to DFA?" The answer was easy. "Blaine Lourd."

I found it fascinating that Lourd himself believes that in a perfect world there wouldn't be any stock brokers or mutual fund managers. But he says the world is not perfect. Lourd says people need to believe that there's a person, and that this person knows what to do with investors' portfolios better than they do. To the investor, that person might as well be Blaine Lourd.

What about investors that systematically beat the market? The article emphasizes that this simply is not the case. If, by some miracle, an investor comes along that can beat the market, it is the individual investor, not investors as a whole, who will benefit. Remember that good information given to too many people becomes bad information.

You are sold on the premise of the importance of the markets, though at no time in the article does Lourd talk about the important economic function he was contributing to, other than his own. That's what the media's role is all about. They tell a story every day about today's stock returns. As the article states, "It's businessman's pornography." If anyone from Wall Street calls you up with financial advice, you should be very afraid. But it isn't fear that promotes investors to embrace DFA: it's greed.

At the end of the profile, Lourd pulls out a chart on one of DFA's funds, (just one, because it wouldn't be beneficial for him to reveal true financial statistics) and shows how it outperformed Warren Buffett's Hathaway funds.

There's a very nice picture of Lourd in the profile projecting a smiling, trustworthy face. He is very smart and handsome. Obviously he projects a winning personality. Lourd talks about how bad it is, but he keeps getting better and better at what he's doing. It proves that he doesn't really care. He is neither unique nor different. He's one of thousands. The photo of him reading the sports page, while a monkey reads the stock quotes, is as accurate a description of the market as the article itself. And yet, he's still in the game.

The article is yet another example of how the greatest scam artists will tell you what they do is a scam, but still convince you that what they're working on now is legit.

11

Publicly Traded Companies
Are tThe Worst Enemy of Private Companies

W hy am I talking about public and private companies in a book about markets? I believe a majority of
investors who purchase shares of a publicly traded company
have no idea what an overall negative impact their action
has on their own community. Publicly traded companies
are harmful to the economy on both a local and national
scale.

Think about it for a moment. How do publicly traded
companies run private companies out of business? Most people believe behemoth-sized companies buy goods in higher
volume at lower prices, at the same time offering significantly
reduced prices to consumers. They also claim that vigorous
competition is part of a capitalistic society. The problem is
that neither one of these are accurate.

The main reason publicly traded companies run private companies out of business is through the use of free capital provided by shareholders.

Publicly traded companies claim to be at a disadvantage as they have more regulations to satisfy. They have to spend more on accounting, bureaucratic paperwork, and filing reports, such as the 10-K reports filed with the Security and Exchanges Commission. It is also argued that publicly traded companies are under more pressure to "make the numbers" because they have shareholders waiting for a return on their investment. Private corporations don't have to disclose such information and are not bound by the same regulations as publicly traded companies.

The seven ways publicly traded companies are bad for your community:

1. Publicly traded companies have a significant advantage in raising capital.
2. Company profits leave your community.
3. Company pyramids the wealth to the CEOs.
4. Company eliminates local competition.
5. Company eliminates convenience.
6. Company lobbyists control campaign financing.
7. Money you invest to buy stock in the company leaves the community.

These so-called advantages of a private company are minor compared to the major obstacles facing them in going up against a publicly traded company.

Here's a simple example: A private owner goes to the bank and gets a business loan for $10,000 for ten years at 6 percent interest. At the end of the loan period, the owner would have repaid the principal of $10,000, plus $3,000 interest for $13,000 total.

A publicly traded company that sold $10,000 worth of shares doesn't have to pay the capital back, and only has an option to pay dividends that average out to about 1 percent a year. At the end of ten years, the company would have paid out $1000 ($100/year for ten years) in dividends. For our example, the hypothetical company was generous enough to pay dividends. Some companies choose not to pay any dividends at all.

The private company is out the principal, plus interest, totaling $13,000. The publicly traded company only loses the dividend, and leaves them with $9,000 of free capital. The publicly traded company has $9,000 of free capital, plus the private company has had to repay $13,000. The publicly traded company has a $22,000 advantage with the added benefit of free capital. Now, take that $10,000 and make it $10,000,000 and this shows the enormous advantage publicly traded companies have over private companies.

What other negative qualities do publicly traded companies present to the community? Due to their access to a large amount of free capital, a national retail chain (NRC) comes to a town with an instantly recognizable name. They build a gigantic store overnight and hold a carnival-like grand opening with severely slashed sale prices.

Good will, along with a customer base the private company has built over the years, is immediately undermined. This is not done with profit or efficiency. These mega-stores are built on free capital. This process has forced many privately owned companies to close their doors.

I built a company from scratch, and I will tell you that competition is a vital function of Capitalism. I also believe competition is the consumers' greatest asset, until the goal of publicly traded companies becomes elimination of competition. When a national retail chain comes into town and builds a mega-store, they are an immediate threat to locally owned competition, (drug stores, hardware stores, grocery stores, shoe stores, dress shops, etc).

As these smaller concerns fall, the consumer has fewer and fewer shopping choices. The variety of products available is confined to those offered by the mega-store. The mega-store becomes a magnet for shoppers in small surrounding towns, and, locally owned stores soon fail there. Within a very short time small-town consumers lose their freedom of choice. They are forced to travel to NRC's centralized location to buy essential products available in the store.

In many cases, it's the business practices of the NRC that drive manufacturers out of business. They're so big that they can dictate terms of payment, short pays, short order, and delayed paying suppliers on invoices, so that it forces suppliers into a "no-win" situation. Here's an example: a supplier bills the NRC $10,000 for their goods. The NRC takes up to ninety days to pay the invoice, then when the payment arrives, the invoice is modified to include added "charges" the NRC incurred, and the check is for $7,500. The supplier has a choice to fight to get the other $2,500, at the risk of legal fees and possibly losing the NRC as a client, or simply to accept the losses and continue the relationship at a reduced profit margin. This is known as a "short pay."

Publicly traded companies have significant advantages that create an unlevel playing field

In some cases, the NRC dictates both to the consumer and supplier. If the NRC decides not to carry the product, the customer has no place to buy it, and the supplier has no one to sell it to so the NRC is actually limiting choice to their consumers by controlling the market. In a free market, the consumer should always be in control. In this case, it's taken out of the hands of the consumer and put in the hands of the NRC.

There is no motivation for the NRC to purchase products locally or even nationally. It has forced some large manufacturers to relocate out of the United States to lower production costs below what can realistically occur in the United States at the cost of our local manufacturers.

On the local level, the NRC takes all of their administrative, management, and marketing functions and profit and moves it to their home office. The money that local people spend on shares of the NRC goes to the home office and is not reinvested in the community. The NRC, in many instances, pays their employees a wage that is lower than average, reducing the standard of living in the town.

In a privately owned company, the management, marketing, and administrative expenses, as well as the profit, would remain in the community with local people put to work. Suppliers have more opportunities to sell their goods. Consumers decide what and where to purchase. Stronger local economies are created with more options for consumers and for suppliers.

Why are private companies more efficient than publicly traded companies? Private companies have to earn a profit. Borrowed money has to be repaid with those profits. Owners who don't build a wide customer base, who don't offer customer services and desirable products don't earn a profit. There will be no golden parachute or obscene performance bonus for these business owners.

You see the enormous advantage that publicly traded companies have over the private sector. With free capital, they can work on a much smaller profit margin—or no margin at all. So they can discount their products and gain the advantage over their private sector competitors.

They accomplish this feat at the expense of the shareholders.

More importantly, a private company is most likely locally owned, and it conducts a majority of its business within the community. Customer good will is paramount. The publicly traded company is far less likely to invest in the community. The community has a false sense of security due to the appearance of the publicly traded company with its glitzy store, promise of employment, and foremost, cheap prices. As I said before, the search for security is the greatest threat to our freedom.

The publicly traded company has to answer to the scrutiny of Wall Street, which spends countless hours and money analyzing, speculating, and anticipating what the quarterly reports will show next. Despite what we know about the con, companies pay special interest and react to what they think will result in a more favorable report.

I'm going to show you why today's business practices are not only bad for the private sector, but for the economy as a whole. As we discussed, publicly traded companies have more expenses due to the nature of their corporate structure. They also have to contend with increased rules and regulations, while showing a consistent profit to continue with business as usual.

Publicly traded companies don't repay the collected principal provided by shareholders. To level the playing field with private companies, publicly owned companies would have to pay approximately 12 percent dividends. Shareholders would be ecstatic, and private companies would have a better chance to compete.

This 12 percent sounds like a lot of money, but since the investors provided the principal with no guarantee of a return, this does not seem like an unreasonable option. Now, how many publicly traded companies do you know that pay out a consistent 12 percent dividend? Since this would put publicly traded companies on the same level as private sector companies where there would be true competition, it won't happen any time soon.

With all of the misinformation about benefits to the community that NRC brings, the consumer ultimately pays the price. The community loses in the end. When inefficient companies run more efficient companies out of business, it has an overall negative effect on the economy.

Reality—CEOs have an ace up their sleeve

The Federal Government bailout of Fannie Mae, Freddie Mac, AIG, and Lehman Brothers will cost taxpayers $5 trillion (yes, that's a 't') or more. Yet Freddie Mac CEO Richard Syron was paid $14.5 million in 2007, including a $2.2 million "performance bonus." Syron has taken home $38 million total from Freddie Mac in the past five years. Fannie Mae CEO Daniel Mudd got $14.2 million in 2007, Lehman Brothers' CEO Dick Fund made $490 million cashing in stocks and stock options before the company went broke.

The scandalous aspect of all of this is that this is just a small example of excessive CEO salaries involving companies that lost money and cost their shareholders and employees countless amounts of money and hardship, while the CEO rides his "golden parachute" safely away.

The CEO of a publicly traded company is given opportunities to make a fortune by taking advantage of stock options being issued in their own company. The argument is that by getting stock options as part of their overall compensation package, the CEO is motivated to make the company more successful to bring up the stock price. But, if a CEO simply wants to make as much money as possible from the stock options, it doesn't always have to occur from the success of the company.

It doesn't always have to be in the best interest of the CEO for their company to be successful. Here's a hypothetical scenario of how a CEO is able to manipulate the system to their advantage. A CEO's company (Company X) has shares listed on the NYSE with a published value of $20/share, and the CEO, along with a group of insiders, want Company X's stocks to drop to a published value of $10/share.

The CEO puts a secret plan in action to intentionally make the company look bad through poor performance and excess spending. The CEO, through a series of executive decisions, cuts the sales force, increases the budget for unnecessary personnel and equipment. Increased expenses and decreased sales raise costs and lower profits. It's possible even to manipulate statistics to artificially deflate the value of the company.

When Company X suddenly shows a dramatic loss in profits, the stock drops to a published value of $10/share as a result of the perception of poor performance.

The CEO is eventually forced out through retirement or termination. Either way he leaves with a lavish severance package that includes stock options to purchase a million shares of Company X stock at its current published value of $10/share.

The outgoing CEO has confidence in the new CEO, who has a reputation for turning companies around. Let's say the shares increase to a published value of $15/share, he can still buy them at $10/share and automatically has a $5/share profit advantage over other investors. If he buys it under value, it devalues the other shareholders that purchased it at a published value of $15/share.

The former CEO decides to exercise the option to buy a million shares of stock at $10/share. Company X now has $10 million of additional capital.

The new CEO of Company X immediately builds market confidence by cutting the payroll and reducing expenses as well as increasing the sales force and instituting new sales programs. Company X once again shows growth and profit through this well-executed plan. The stock increases in published value up to $25/share.

In this scenario, the former CEO pockets money at any point as long as investors purchase Company X shares at a published price above $10/share. The CEO then decides to sell, making a million dollars profit for every dollar the share goes up above $10/share.

This may be an overly simplistic example, but I can assure you that the level of deception that goes on is far more complex and devious. The results are the same.

It's scandalous that publicly traded companies are allowed to pay stock options and excessive salaries to CEOs whether they deserved them or not. Employees, without insider information, shouldn't accept stock options as part of their benefit package. CEO's that have insider information should be denied stock options in their own companies as it creates an obvious conflict-of-interest. The Security and Exchange Commission has required increased disclosure of CEO compensation packages, but this has had only a slight effect.

The key here is that investors and employees lose because the excess salaries paid to CEO's come directly from the shareholders with no accountability. The board of directors doesn't care—it's not their money. The SEC allows boards of directors free reign to set salaries as they see fit. The real scandal, as we discussed earlier, is that CEOs are rewarded as much for the poor performance of their company as for a strong performance.

The myth of the "compassionate CEO"

Bill Gates of Microsoft made news in late 2007 by encouraging his colleagues in the business world to become more of a compassionate CEO, directing more of their profits to help developing third-world countries. Mr. Gates, in the past, has committed himself to give away most of his fortune to those in need overseas. While, at first glance, this appears commendable there's a problem with this plan. Microsoft didn't pay dividends until 2003, after reportedly being threatened with a 39.5 percent corporate tax for excessive profits, and the dividend payout, according to the information on the Microsoft investor relations website (as of October 1, 2008) is approximately 2 percent. At this rate, it would take fifty years to pay shareholders for their principal.

Gates needs to pay dividends to the shareholders who helped make him a billionaire before he starts giving it away, domestically or overseas. He's not giving away his money but giving away his shareholders' money, without their permission.

The bottom line is that by playing the stock market and buying shares in a publicly traded company, you are handing the company money you won't get back for them to use as free capital to spend as they wish. But, more importantly, you are contributing to an increasing problem of these publicly traded companies pushing out the private companies and reducing choices for the consumer.

12
Yearly Personal Reports

Throughout this book, I have repeatedly asked why the brokers and exchanges are not required to produce any reports of investors' money. I think it's time that we demand from our elected officials that all participants have to provide full accountability of how much money investors have spent out-of-pocket on investments, fees, commissions, and estimated taxes.

Here's my simple solution: The following three reports would show a detailed accounting of each individual investors' money, brokers' performance as a whole, and the exchange with all participants as a whole. It would be required that the broker and exchange reports be published annually and available to anyone upon request, while the yearly personal report would be confidential.

I did not factor in the negative cash flow of the taxes collected or deducted by the IRS. These charts would go a long way toward providing investors with an honest accountability of their money.

If these reports were required and made public today, how many of you would still be confident in the markets, and would this book would still be necessary?

Broker Performance Report on Total Clients

(Broker) Name: _____

Firm: _____

Year: _____ Signature: _____

Number of clients with positive Cash Flow:_____ Total amount in pocket: $ _____	Number of clients with negative Cash Flow:_____ Total amount in pocket: $ _____
This report is made public every year.	

Exchanges Performance Report on Total Clients

Name:_____

Year: _____

Year: _____

Number of clients with positive Cash Flow:_____ Total amount in pocket: $ _____	Number of clients with negative Cash Flow:_____ Total amount in pocket: $ _____
This report is made public every year.	

Yearly Personal Report

Name: _____

Acct #: _____

Out-of-pocket expenses: $ _____

In-pocket expenses: $ _____

A. Out-of-Pocket expenses:	**B. In-pocket expenses:**
Purchases $ _____	Sales $ _____
Fees: $ _____	Settlements $ _____
Commissions: $ _____	Dividends $ _____
Total A: $ _____	Total B: $ _____
Total money out of pocket (N): $ _____ (Negative cash flow)	**Total money in pocket (P): $ _____ (Positive cash flow)**
If A is bigger than B Subtract B from A	*If B is bigger than A Subtract A from B*

This information is an accurate accounting of the client's yearly transactions.

Broker Name: _____

Signature: _____

(Note: This does not factor in taxes) Each year, the exchanges would be required to provide this information to each client.

13

You May Not Beat the System, but You Can Quit Losing Money

I'm sixty-eight years old, and I've spent the last four years trying to understand the stock market and commodity markets. It comes down to this:

Wall Street's entire function is as a revenue-generating organization. Since they produce no tangible products, they are entirely dependent on you placing and keeping your money in motion. When you do that, a majority of time the Wall Street firms win and investors lose.

As I discussed earlier, the majority of books that propose a way to "beat the markets" are written by people who make their fortunes by selling books, CD's, DVD's and seminars, not by following any system they promote. Therefore, I have no "magic solution." There is no way to beat the system. That doesn't mean that you should put your money in a mattress. Simply put, the purpose of the book was to tell you the dangers of the markets, and expose the pitfalls of Wall Street and the commodities exchanges, and show that you are playing a losing game.

So, where should you put your money? I'm not an investment advisor, nor a "financial guru," but it's easy to see that we are a country drowning in debt. We buy houses we can't afford, have multiple credit cards with increasing spending limits, and surround ourselves in conspicuous consumption. We are so willing to live on credit that it's almost funny to think that we are handing ourselves or our children a future through 401 (k) or pensions.

My dad told me years ago that a man who has money in his pocket will eat that night. One who doesn't might go hungry. I may be a common man, but I went to the school of hard knocks and graduated at the head of the class and majored in CM (counting money). It was this real-life education that led me to lose faith in what I had been told or taught. I followed my money and did the math. Facts are facts.

What I'm recommending to you is not any plan for investments, as I've showed you the stock and commodities markets were not designed for that purpose. First of all, here's what I recommend:

GET OUT OF DEBT!

If you're going to invest, invest in yourself. Pay off your mortgage, get rid of your credit cards, become debt free. This will likely take time and discipline, but if you take what you're putting into a 401 (k) or other retirement plan and pay off your debts, that will put you in a much stronger position than any investment risk.

In addition, it will teach you the discipline to plan for your later years with much more confidence than just hoping your 401 (k) will be there when you retire. And before you scoff at that notion, remember this: More than likely, if you are reading this book, you are part of, or will see the results of the largest group of people in human history to reach retirement age. Those people will all be cashing in their 401 (k)s and buyers for those stocks will be needed. Will Wall Street guarantee those investments? Will the government? And if so, at what percentage of the perceived value you thought you had initially, and how much of your taxes will go to secure these payments?

I invested my money in starting a company and buying land. People have purchased tangible objects like land, classic cars, bonds, T-bills, bank CD's, etc. Your expected return will be lower, but you are participating in a true "investment." Investing in something hoping to make a huge return is another way of saying that you're gambling.

If you are debt-free and have money to invest, while I'm not a financial advisor, here is what I would recommend:

- place $100,000 or the maximum federally insured amount, into a CD, to have some money that will always be secure. Your bank then can use that money to invest in your community by making loans for small businesses, home loans and personal loans;
- be wary of gold, art and similar investments that can be just as risky as stocks;

- forget about commodities options, short selling, derivatives and similar complex investments that even specialists don't fully understand. Let me put it this way, if Warren Buffett doesn't understand derivatives, you think you do?;
- ignore anything that's "securitized" (assets packaged into securities, there is no chance you can evaluate the underlying assets);
- it's OK to purchase real estate or tangible property, but only if your plan is to hold it for many years. Don't purchase real estate, or any form of real property, thinking you will "flip" it for a huge profit, you'll have more payments than buyers;
- anyone promising "confidential tax avoidance strategies" or "a once in a lifetime opportunity" is someone you should run away from as fast as possible.

As I discussed earlier, the impact of large publicly traded companies on local communities is robbing the country of the entrepreneurial spirit that makes this country great. By smartly investing in your community, you will build wealth and build the confidence of a new generation of business leaders.

But what if you want to invest on Wall Street?

Fine, you've been warned. But to recap, this is what we've learned about buying and selling shares in publicly traded companies and contracts in the commodities contracts:

- It is a scam designed to take money from the pockets of investors and transfer it to the pockets of the few.
- It's gambling as much as any casino, except Wall Street's games are crooked.
- It is a minus-sum game.
- Not only is it a minus-sum game, but a majority of investors as a whole lose money.
- No records are kept or required to determine the exact amount of investors that lose money.
- Prices are not determined on any mathematical or scientific formula.
- Prices are created on the consensus of the buyers and sellers trying to predict an unpredictable.
- The prices change constantly.
- Investors can buy and sell by the second.
- This buying and selling creates volatility.
- The volatility creates motion.
- The motion takes money out of pockets of investors and puts money into the pockets of Wall Street.
- This volatility makes it possible for investors to believe they can turn a little money into a lot of money quickly.

This system was developed and perfected over the years by Wall Street using illusion and deception. They designed this scam to separate generations of Americans from their money without having any accountability or prosecution.

To put this system into place, Wall Street had to change the reality that the markets are gambling and to create the perception that the markets are a vital economic function for the masses. To do this, they had to concoct an image that investors, by participating, can:

- make money;
- achieve financial security;
- contribute to a vital and important economic function;
- take responsibility for their own losses.

In the process, Wall Street firms knew they had to develop a system so complex that the news media, the academic community, the federal officials, and the public wouldn't understand it while they accepted it without question. The system itself was designed to such an extent that the burden of responsibility is placed on the investors to be accountable for their losses. As it was so complex and difficult to understand, the federally elected officials needed to set up self-regulated commissions to oversee and manage the markets. They effectively put the fox in charge of the hen house.

If you invest in the markets, understand that the regulatory commissions are not designed to support you. The role of the regulatory commissions of the commodities market and stock markets are to design rules and regulations to:

- ensure the winners get their money;
- ensure the success of the organization;

- ensure losers in the markets have no legal recourse;
- ensure that no records be kept or required that would endanger the success of the organization.

The commissions set up rules preventing investors who lose money from seeking retribution or holding the exchanges liable for their losses. Through this process, the investor is conditioned to accept all responsibility for losses. As long as the rules are followed, there's no recourse for justice through the exchanges, and the investor ultimately must live with the results. By accepting responsibility for their losses, investors fail to seek action from our federally elected officials to force the exchanges to provide full accountability for investors' money.

Once they got control of the system through self-regulation, Wall Street worked to prevent any rules that would provide full disclosure and accountability. They could avoid keeping any records or publishing any statistics that would hold them accountable to investors. Nothing detrimental to the system is disclosed. They are now in control of a system designed to ensure successful market exchanges. Until that is changed, there is no motivation from Wall Street to change their practices.

Through deception, Wall Street succeeded in making you believe the illusion that investors are not gambling, but they are performing a legitimate economic function to secure their financial futures. The news media, academic world, and federally elected officials all fell in line and promoted that premise without question.

Next, Wall Street created a series of gambling games that enticed investors as a whole into thinking they could turn a little money into a lot of money without effort. In order to maintain the illusion that investors were investing, they added terms of value to their games. The games were disguised as a business function when in fact it was simply a contest where an investor tries to outguess other investors in predicting a nonpredictable.

Wall Street created a system that ensures that the brokers and exchanges have a constant flow of money coming in through motion. As Warren Buffet's Fourth Law of Motion says: "As motion increases, investors' returns decreases." The more times you invest, the more money you lose.

This creates a minus-sum game for investors. While this should be obvious to even the most experienced investors, they persist in believing the deception that the markets are a zero-sum gain. When you add in fees, commissions, taxes, and other expenses, investors as a whole wind up with less money in their pocket at the end of the day then before they started. As the market presently functions, all investors, as a whole, will lose money in time. And, as we've discussed, the records to specify how many people lose money and how much are not kept or required.

Mathematically, more losers, than winners, guarantee that markets will survive. We've been sold on the illusion of "published value," when in reality there is no money to back it up. Unless you find another investor to pay you to take over the contract, your paper is worthless. The term "perceived value" is what you believe you can get in return, but it has no basis for actual worth. Both of these terms are words of illusion with investors placed in a very dangerous position.

At the end of the day, I don't see why you would even try to play Wall Street's games as they are currently designed when they are so thoroughly designed to generate revenue for brokerage houses at the expense of investors. Are you the person who stops at the shell game on the street and is sure the next $20 will be the one where you guess under which shell has the ball?

Can Wall Street ever be reformed?

You'll hear the argument that as a free-enterprise system, the best thing for Wall Street to correct itself is to let the markets correct themselves without government intervention. And normally, I'd agree. But Congress and the media are caught up in Wall Street's propaganda and are willing to reward poor business practices. Honestly, the best thing I can recommend for addressing Wall Street is to get you to quit losing money in the market. If you did that, it would correct itself with no Congressional intervention. Unfortunately, it's hard for the markets to correct themselves when Congress and the Federal Reserve is ready with taxpayer bailout money for every Wall Street firm facing extinction.

For once, those who are taken advantage of by the markets are in control. This is area in which we don't need any new laws or help from our federal elected officials. The only sure way for investors to quit losing money is to quit participating in the two largest con games in U.S. history . . . the stock market and commodity markets. By taking money out of the pockets of the few and keeping it in your pockets and your community, how can that be bad in the long-term for the economy?

But, as I've said before, just because there are rules and laws doesn't mean they are good rules or good laws. If our federal elected officials were to actually work for the people and pass a couple of laws to greatly reduce the gambling aspect from the markets, that may establish confidence in the market. Here's what I recommend:

- Limit the ability to trade from hundreds of times a year to twelve times per year.
- Force the exchanges to enact rules that state that once you purchase a share or contract, you can sell them at anytime. However, you must hold it for at least thirty days to reap a profit.
- Eliminate margins on the commodity exchanges. This would eliminate the gambling aspect of earning approximately twenty times the true value.
- Require true accountability and disclosure from firms about where our money is and who is making and losing money.

These simple reforms would remove the gambling aspect from the markets by eliminating the lure of turning a little money into a lot of money quickly. And if you choose to take the risk, then you know in advance.

Since Wall Street employs hundreds of thousands of people across several industries, there will be every effort to do whatever it takes in the name of self-preservation. I expect to be attacked, questioned, threatened, and dismissed as being "anti-American" or a "socialist" by those who will attempt to discredit me. I might be vilified as "anti-American." I will certainly be accused of being ignorant of the system by not presenting a complex and confusing thesis full of dull research in order to impress a few and confuse the many. I will be censured for presenting a doomsday scenario leading to the suggestion that everyone quit buying stock and commodities. It will be said that my philosophies will lead to an economic collapse and a return to the stone-age. To hold on to the status quo, every attempt will be made to scare you with talk about the dangers of a shrinking market.

Now you know what they didn't want you to know. Ignoring or dismissing this is the biggest risk you can take, and it's a losing risk at that.

And where should you put your money? Ultimately, it's up to you, but I would recommend that you become debt-free and don't ever put your money where it's not guaranteed. If you do, you give the money manager the right to steal it without recourse. It comes down to this, do you trust Wall Street with your money?

Me neither.

Appendix One:
Questions Your Broker Won't Answer, with Answers that Your Broker Won't Want to Admit

....

Go ask your broker for a report on investors' money. When you get the runaround, ask these questions:

What is your job as a broker?

What is the average return on investments on public related company stocks?

Are there guarantees that I won't lose my money?

Are there any guarantees that I can sell my shares or contacts?

What is the average dividend paid on outstanding stock?

Where does the money come from when I sell my shares or contacts?

What is the average life of a publicly traded company on the stock market?

If I lose money, whose fault is it?

Does your job as a broker depend on investors losing money?

What do companies do with the money they get from investors? Do they pay it back?

Why does it say on the stock certificates, they "have no par value?"

When I lose my money by selling my share or contracts, do brokers and money managers get penalized or reprimanded by the Security and Exchange Commission (SEC) or the National Futures Association (NFA)?

How are prices on shares or contacts determined?

How is margin money in the commodities market divided up?

What percentage of investors make money?

Can I go to the bank and borrow money to buy shares or contacts?

Is there any accounting system on how stock prices or commodities contracts are established? Do you keep records on investors money?

Are CEO stock options a positive or negative to the average Investor?

The last time I checked, a seat on the NYSE sold for $4 million. Does a NYSE seat holder hold any advantages over the average investor? What about seats on the mercantile exchanges?

Is trading shares or contracts a zero-sum gain? With expenses, does it become a minus-sum gain?

The stock market collects money for companies that they don't pay back. Brokers and money managers make money. The IRS makes money along with 5 percent of investors. Where does all of that money come from?

If losers quit losing, what would happen to the markets?

Why aren't brokers and money managers required to keep records of investors' money and publish the statistics?

The published "value" of all outstanding stock is approximately $15 trillion. How much of that money is put back into our economy through investors?

What percentage of commodities contracts is actually delivered?

Is an investor's cash flow worse when the market is open or closed?

Do you have any idea how much money investors have made or lost in the commodity market and the stock market in the prior year?

How many new stock shares were issued in the past calendar year?

If, in a 401 (k) you began playing at age eighteen, and you retire at age sixty-five, which is forty-seven years, what is the percentage of publicly traded companies would last for those forty-seven years?

Can you tell me how much money all your investors made as a whole last year?

At the end of each day, do investors as a whole have less money in their pocket than they started with?

How much money did investors lose in selling publicly traded stocks or commodities contracts to other investors?

What was the percentage of losers to winners in the markets? Can you tell me how much money your clients lost last year?

These are the answers you should receive:

"Nine-out-of-ten investors will lose some or all of their money."

"You are entering into a game of chance. You are trying to out-predict other investors."

"There is no possible way investors as a whole can make money."

"When stock is issued, the company keeps the money and doesn't pay it back."

"If all things were equal, all investors would lose money in time."

"The markets are supported by losers. If the losers quit losing money, I would be out of a job."

"If you make money selling your stock, the money comes from another investor, not the company."

"To investors as a whole, there are only two positive cash flows, company buy backs (approximately 1 percent of the time) and dividends (paying approximately 1–3 percent)"

"No one knows how all of that margin money is divided up."

"I don't keep performance records so I can't tell you if my clients made money or lost money investing."

"My job is to keep your money moving, not to worry about your losses."

"I make my money off fees and commissions, not the success of your investments."

"I make money, even if you don't."

"When you buy shares or contracts there are no guarantees that you can sell them or what price you will receive."

"You are my source of income, but if you lose money selling your shares or contracts, it is your own fault."

"Investors buying and selling shares and contracts is a zero-sum gain. This means that at the end of the day, investors as a whole have no more or no less money than they started with."

"When you add commissions and transaction fees, it becomes a minus-sum gain. This means that at the end of the day, investors lose money."

"Only positive cash flow to shareholders is considered dividends. Dividends are less then 1 percent."

"If companies buy back their shares, that is considered a positive cash flow to investors. Company buy backs are approximately one percent."

"CEO stock options are a negative to average investors."

"People with a seat on the exchanges have a built-in advantage over the average investor. If they didn't why would they pay for the seat?"

"The average life of a publicly traded company is eight years."

"You as an investor pay the wages for exchanges, brokers and money managers."

"The IRS takes money from the winners."

"The job of the SEC and NFA is to see that exchanges are successful. Losers are responsible for losses, not the exchanges, brokers or money managers."

3 1170 00805 0936